Snow

BETSY HOWIE

For Christine —
where have you gone?
I miss you a blizzard's
worth.
Betsy Howie

Harcourt Brace & Company
NEW YORK   SAN DIEGO   LONDON

Library of Congress Cataloging-in-Publication Data
Howie, Betsy.
Snow: a novel/Betsy Howie.
p.   cm.
ISBN 0-15-100273-8
I. Title.
PS3558.O919S65   1998
813.54—dc21   97-29412

Text set in Sabon
Designed by Carolyn Deacy
Printed in the United States of America
First edition

A C E D B

In memory
of
Aralee
whose search for her own bear made possible mine.
I see you missing in so many faces.

Contents

The author gratefully acknowledges the help
and guidance of many. Among them:

Ruth Danon for finding the structure in the chaos

*Dr. Healey and the MSKCC folks for taking the
chaos out of the structure*

Dad for the will

Mom for the willingness

Matt and Karen for Matt and Karen

*Peter for telling me about Lurie and of course,
Lurie for Rubin, and of course, Rubin for
Candace, and of course, Candace*

*Maggie for Rob Weisbach, and of course Rob for
Elaine, and of course, Elaine*

*Ann and Laura G. and Judy and Laura M. and
Maggie (again) and Jane and Paula for talking*

Denise for listening

and of course, of course, FJT.

If you don't know why, don't nobody.

ONE

The Wait and See

I DREAMT OF CATS escaping out open windows, two nights in a row. One fell several stories from my apartment. One rode the wind, on the roof of my mobile home. All of them were my children, clear acts of rebellion. I awoke the first morning and yelled for my mother, who did not hear me. Then I yelled for my husband, who came quickly, concerned and confused. On Sunday I awoke and stripped two chairs of three generations of bad greens and blues.

On Saturday we bought a secretary with glass doors and real drawers. We, my husband and I, carefully spread newspapers on the rug, the most expensive thing I ever bought while living in my studio apartment on the Lower East Side, the apartment where Clyde the cat left one day with a leap from the window onto the fire escape and was never seen or heard from again. We, my husband and I, worked for three hours with steel wool, soap and chemicals, and old tattered boy underwear. We made little circles with the cleaners so as not to disturb the grain. The dirt ran off in rivers. The secretary transformed into real furniture, dark and tall.

I used to get all my furniture off the street. Nine years ago

I spotted a wonderful old chair on Bowery. I offered the panhandler who was seated on it a five-dollar bill to stand up. Last night, as my husband disappeared into a photo album of dead people looking young given to him by his grandmother, I spread newspaper in the living room and scrubbed the chair for the first time. The dirt ran off in rivers.

Things are getting very clean around here and cats are deserting like rats from a sinking ship.

THIS MORNING IS TYPICAL. I fight to wake up. I fight to turn off the TV. I fight to not buy cigarettes. They're so good with coffee. I have things to do; things that I must do for money, things that I should do for art, things that I want to do. I try and get them done in that order. I try to make the day go from pain to pleasure. I want to go for cigarettes. I want to clean the rug. I want to make video art. I want to shop the grocery store. I want to sing with the stereo. I want to figure out dinner. I want to strip the wicker. I want to win a Pulitzer prize and I want to be a movie star. I should speak to Doug.

We fought yesterday, Doug and I. Our friendship has a long history of badgering and poking but we've never actually lashed out with no smile quickly following. I am uncertain how to proceed. Yesterday, when I hung up the phone, I had chairs to paint but today I'm surrounded by finished furniture and nine or ten hours until dinner.

There was a dream last night. I slid down a wall, collapsed, sitting on a floor, knees up, butt and feet together. The pain was low, beneath my belly, female pain so intense that I could not call out for help. I pulled in air with short wide sucks as my fists clenched and released. I tried to find a reasonable level of tolerance for this pain. People were near but they were behind doors, they were talking, they were turned. They were busy with important things that required suits and heels. They moved quick.

Doug said, "Well, excuse me for saying so, but you live in Brooklyn and make meat loaf every night, if you know what I mean." And I said, "Fuck off, to that, Doug." He said, "I'm sorry, did I offend you?" When I hung up the phone, the writer in me paced and ranted, the maker of meat loaf cried.

The phone just rang, it was my husband. He says Doug and I are just going through a thing. He says it will all be OK. I'm going for cigarettes and I'll pick up some milk because there's one more cup of coffee left in the pot.

"CRYING, AT THREE O'CLOCK IN THE MORNING . . ." The words of an old song played in my head as I leaned against the counter edge with my head on my arms. I tried to visualize the Advil capsules breaking apart and being swept under by the raging current of my bloodstream, being whisked away to form a block between the pain in my uterus and the synapses in my brain. I tried to breathe deeply, drop my shoulders.

Last night my husband and I drove Kate home at eleven o'clock after an evening out. She had a date at 11:30 with the Pakistani man she met when he leaned out his car door window and said she was the most beautiful woman he'd ever seen. The night before last, she sat up all night drinking water from crystal with the man she met at a paint store. She told me he threw the wineglass out an open window with perfect precision. It sailed cleanly through the air, making noise just when it shattered in the courtyard three stories below. I knew the recollection would make Kate shiver and breathe deeply and it did. She lives on East 4th Street between Avenues A and B, only one block from my old apartment. She says life is to get dressed up in.

I am shifting in my chair, trying to find comfort, trying to appease my uterus without sitting directly on the pimples that have begun to appear in recent months. This pain is worse than it used to be. I remember that I used to visualize one cut at my belly button and another level with my pelvic bone. I imagined removing that section and shelving it until it behaved. But now the pain has spread. It has intensified, it makes my legs ache and my head throb. I suspect that my uterus is angry, having done its job every month for so many years and having nothing to show for it. It is gathering its force and will use it against me.

My husband idled the car as Kate passed through the doors of her building. A punker, who followed her inside, held the door. I watched as she moved quickly toward the stairs. There was the unmistakable hitch in her walk, the vibrating air of a girl with a late-night date, and the ache in my body moved closer to my heart. I used to live right around the corner. I used to stay out all night.

My friend Chris knows with near certainty just how many eggs she has left. They are represented by small circles drawn on a paper that sits by her bed. She marks them off with a little teardrop every time she loses another.

I MADE A CHART YESTERDAY. It has eight headings across the top, the projects I care about. It runs downward according to the days of the week. I soften with each *X*, when I have done what I said I would do, keeping my promise.

The weather turned cold three days ago. Summer lost its grip. That smell that permeates from one season to the next became winter's and my nerves turned on edge, knowing the promises I have made for the spring, watching the time push on.

Last night my husband and I had friends to our home for dinner. At midnight, having cleaned our new wedding gift dishes, we went to bed. The dream was a rehearsal, a scene from *The Sound of Music*. Over and over, escaping through a graveyard, wrapped in a blanket, singing. We couldn't get it right so it just kept happening, endlessly, the same words and music and movement. Nothing changed, people yelled, people walked backward. I itched under my blanket, I sang the wrong tune, I went off pitch. There was no air.

Last week I danced on the roof at Doug's house, stoned and inspired by the blue sky and fresh air. Doug followed me with a video camera. Bells tolled, I twirled, a breeze blew, and we laughed ridiculously hard. When I recounted this to Kate, day before yesterday, she said, "But that was when warm weather was still a possibility."

MONEY IS TIGHT RIGHT NOW. That's what my husband said as we lay in bed last night staring straight up at the ceiling. I worked to stay quiet, to not speak my mind, to not say things I know I shouldn't. I rolled over and made tiny movements with my eyes, outlining the flowers on the worn flannel sheets. He sighed with noise. He has trouble sleeping. I sleep like the dead. It is my responsibility to be fair after midnight, to not rile his mind too much. I pushed his leg to his side of the bed and pulled the quilt tight around my neck.

During the summer of 1984, Kate and I worked the midnight shift at a cherry factory in northern Michigan. We started at ten o'clock at night, we finished at six in the morning. We wore white aprons, hair nets, and plastic gloves as we stood watch over a series of conveyor belts that ran cherries continuously from huge wooden crates loaded by forklifts to plastic buckets that were loaded onto trucks. We stared down at the red streak, plucked out the pitted or shriveled, dropped them in the stream of water that ran alongside the belt. Those cherries became pie.

We had one break, though Kate snuck away regularly on the hour to the ladies' room, motion sickness. At two in the morning, half the women would back away from the belts, stretch. They would walk to the parking lot, where they would climb into the cabs of pickup trucks, kiss their husbands, who were on break from the forklifts, and unwrap their cheese sandwiches, lean their heads back against the glass of the rear windows, close their eyes, and chew.

My husband doesn't want to talk about money. He wants to sit down with paper and find out exactly where we stand. I told him last night, I know where we stand. I have to bring in more money. We pay a thousand dollars in rent, a thousand to his analyst, several hundred more in bills, credit card debt, cat food, and spending money. I need cigarette change.

He turned in bed last night, away from me, wide awake. The tension released slowly, from his back, his legs, his neck. Then he was sleeping. I imagined myself as part of the fabric of America, a wife at night in her bed with her husband, worried about the bills, about the spending and the savings, about keeping the anxiety away from the marriage. Money is tight right now.

Kate and I laughed at each other the first time we saw ourselves in the white uniform of the cherry sorter. We said Lucy and Ethel and talked about buying new dresses. The cherries jammed up along my belt until I understood that some would slide by. I stared at the women who had done this before, smiled at them. I tried to speak to them but then the cherries would jam up. My stomach was tight. My hands were cold. I would alternate positions on my stool, then standing, thinking of America, of Steinbeck and Odets.

My body ached by the end of the shift. The women around me moved quickly and quietly. They stripped off the white, met their husbands in the parking lot, nodded to each other, and pulled out. Kate and I arrived home at 6:30 in the morning. We both fell into a sick sleep and awoke several hours later. We didn't speak. I simply picked up the phone, dialed the factory, and informed the boss that we would not be coming back.

This morning I woke up at nine o'clock. My husband left

some coffee in the pot. It is my routine to wake slowly over coffee, a cigarette, and two episodes of *I Love Lucy*. I am married now. I will work in my office in my apartment for most of the day, making phone calls and faxing press releases. I will weaken and watch a little of *The Guiding Light*. Cherry season is over. I will write, then think about dinner. My husband will come home and it will be Friday night.

THERE'S A SHIFT IN THE AIR when we walk back to the bedroom, when the TV is turned off, when the door is locked, when the rooms go dark. We travel well together, we're very supportive, we take turns with the dishes. We don't have sex.

A river of anxiety runs down our bed. We stare at each other in the light of darkness, though never when the other is looking, searching for a bridge. His touches are clumsy and mine are cold. It's been years since we haven't had to think. The determination behind each new attempt is heroic, the first touch shaky. We remember the first six months, three times a day, and then the decline. I say it was never good, simply enthusiastic. Ray says he never had this problem before me.

He proposed to me two days after I said I was leaving him. He slid a box across a table. I didn't look inside it for three days. When I finally put the ring on my finger, I will always remember how my guts shook, like they used to in my old dreams, jumping off telephone poles. I landed many times in those dreams and have been told that means I've often died. I would wake just after landing, never seeing what came next. I have always wanted to know.

We botched it again on Saturday night. It took most of Sunday to find a way back from the words, the tone. We had to buy a piece of furniture that needed to be stripped. We had to stand next to each other and watch the chemicals eat through the finish, bubble up. We had to scrape the surface with metal. We had to clean it completely and cover it again, with our own color this time, something that revealed the grain, explained the wood. We had to shine the windows and fill the cabinet with the most delicate things we own.

There is a rage in me. It comes up and out of my core, it offers no warning, only a sudden burning above my gut, then it hits the bone, the sternum, the place between my breasts, and then it is in charge. It breaks free, it speaks, it kicks. On Saturday night it left us no time. We braved those first jarring touches and then it blew. I said, "I'm having real trouble with this, I feel like a fucking guinea pig." I got up, got dressed. I said I was going for cigarettes and sat in the living room. I walked back to the bedroom and said we should sleep with other people just to remember what it's supposed to be.

We spoke quietly several hours later. I said I wonder sometimes if something is buried in my mind. He says he is lost and desperate, he is not masculine.

On Friday night I dreamt of the summerhouse on Lake Michigan with its floor-to-ceiling windows that normally look over the water but in my dream they looked into the water. Fish; dead fish, big fish, floated and swam within inches of me. Men filled the room around me, laughed at me.

I threw Ray off the bed once. I can only equate the experience with suffocation, an irrational scrambling for air and space, the anger that comes with the will to survive, its independence and pride. Sometimes, late at night, when I'm sure he is asleep, I stroke his hair, shift my body toward his.

On Saturday morning my husband and I sat at the computer, tried to make sense of our budget. There was no line item for cats so we tallied Sophie and Vinny at $60 a month and put it under "baby-sitting." We are $38 shy this month but it's a bad month, that's what my husband says. The next day we spent $350 on the china cabinet and put it under "medical."

I have a vision of us, years from now, in an apartment so

filled with finished wooden furniture that we are finally forced to live in the only space left open: our bed. My husband and I sat in the kitchen last night, until one in the morning, side by side, my hand in his. We stared at our china cabinet and all that we own that is fragile.

YOU SAY NOTHING THE FIRST TIME YOU HEAR IT. I was a child. Lying in my bed, listening for the noise of long-distance truckers, confirmation that someone else was awake in my world. Things were quiet back then. Alone, awake, and small; that is when I would hear it, the soft yelling. I knew the sound was inside me, it wasn't a physical being. But I didn't know where the sound started or how to make it stop. The soft yelling; purposeful and insistent, it commanded me, informed me. It's like an echo of a scream but it rings so close, it's inside. Vaguely, there was the image of nuns; tall, strong, thin women in their forties and fifties, short tight hair. They moved closer, they never touched. I wouldn't speak about it, never told my parents.

There was the opportunity once, after disobeying my mother by watching *Twilight Zone*. The episode was about a young girl and her dog trapped within the walls of her house. She had fallen out of her bed during sleep and rolled inside the wall. Her parents were trying to get her out but the invisible hole was closing up quickly. Inside walls is a place filled with nothing, endless space, where little girls wander around looking up just slightly, side to side. Little girls cling to their dogs. Every night for weeks after, I screamed in fear that I was going to fall into the wall. Finally, my father said no, and if I did I would land in his closet and he would come for me. He would hear me, and I wanted to ask him at that moment if he also heard the yelling, the soft yelling. But I knew there was no reason, it was something I could not explain. The soft yelling was mine.

I haven't heard the sound in more than fifteen years. I had almost forgotten it, or at least it had turned simpler in memory, until today. As I wrote at my desk, windows closed for the winter, the silence was complete and the yelling came back. I sat motionless, felt the return of something very, very old, recognized it immediately, and wondered how a child could have handled something so terrifying. I buried my pen into my desk and thought if I don't think about it, it will take another form. But I know, looking around me, that my life has not been as quiet as this since childhood.

The yelling has not returned, it did not leave. It is only that I have stopped making so much noise, I can hear it.

I WENT TO A DOCTOR YESTERDAY, rheumatologist. He was supposed to fix the muscle in my leg that was destroyed almost ten years ago, jogging on speed. We sat in his office and he asked me questions. I confessed that I smoke, drink very little, and that I used to jog on speed. I took off my clothes when he told me to and moved my leg as he requested. He pushed the muscle, flexed it. I stood, sat, lay down. He said there was little to be done. The muscle is ruptured, separated from its tendon, it sits in a ball at the top of my thigh and makes problems for the things around it; other muscles, nerves. I asked him about the pain. Sitting, my thigh can rest on the edge of the chair so that the pain is intense, my leg can go numb. He said a cushion might help. I said I could also change positions in the chair but that wasn't the point. Something is wrong with the leg and it needs to be fixed. He smiled a little, cocked his head, and suggested biking shorts.

My grandfather started losing his mind noticeably after my grandmother died. Before that, we called it slipping. His body runs like a Swiss clock. When he falls he heals, and when he falls it is because he is clumsy and not because he thinks up is down, which he does much of any day. He met Ray more than two years before we married, almost six years after college. My grandfather stood, offered his hand to Ray, and asked him what grade he was in. Then he sat and asked for Ray's help in finding Ed Sullivan on the TV. Ray was gentle when he told my grandfather that Ed had been canceled.

As I stepped down from the examining table, the doctor asked me if there was anything else. I didn't know what to say. He asked about blood work. I said no, looked at him. Did he think it was necessary? He asked, when last? I said not since the hepatitis in '85. He suggested a general test, the levels, the counts, the highs, the lows. I said I thought whatever he thought. He said that I was thirty and, generally speaking, he would consider it a good idea for anyone coming into his office, for a thirty-year-old.

Almost two years ago my grandfather was honored as the oldest living All-American University of Michigan basketball player. At the time he said he was happy to be honored though he would have preferred it were for something else. Now I must remind him of the honor, that he walked onto the court at halftime, that he waved to the crowds as they cheered. Last Christmas he asked my mother who I was.

Sometimes I can't believe my husband's name is Ray and I wonder if I'm right, if it really is. It's one of those passing thoughts.

THE DOCTOR WHO HAD NO SOLUTION for the problem in my thigh called this afternoon to inform me that the thigh is not the problem. What is "very serious," in his exact words as I hear them ringing in my head, is the number that came back from the blood test, the one that refers to the cholesterol in my blood. "It's sky high," he said. "It's three hundred." I was calm. I said, "Oh." We discussed a few foods and I thanked him before hanging up.

There is a story that's been told many times since my childhood. At the age of three, my father took me trick-or-treating with the other kids in the neighborhood. As they ran from house to house carrying their bags, tripping on costumes, I walked alongside my father. I would run ahead briefly, then, unable to keep up, would return to my father's hand. Soon after, we began seeing the doctors. I remember these things: long waits with my mother in rooms sparsely set; cold silver furniture; white glass plates on walls; thick pink chalk liquid, forcing it down my throat so the pictures of my heart would tell the doctors why I couldn't run. Then it was the words: *a murmur, a valve, malfunction, antibiotics, wait and see.*

I called my husband after speaking to the doctor; high cholesterol, very serious, another test in a month. He came home early and we went out together to shop for vegetables and skim milk. I put the groceries away on the shelves of my kitchen, reading the labels on all my old cans and cartons. Ray hugged me twice tonight before he sat down to the World Series. My father said we have matching cholesterols, I come by it naturally. My father, the physician, says he's chosen to do very little about it. My father says he knows one thing, this should be the end of my smoking, not another one, not ever.

The "wait and see" of my childhood stretched over ten years. In the time between, I grew accustomed to the steely cold of the stethoscope on my chest and back, to the dry catch of large pills swallowed before dental visits, to the look in a grown-up eye when the words "heart condition" were mentioned. I was the champion of deep breaths, letting them out slow. I considered my precarious existence, imagining Dr. Joe Gannon and his "Medical Center" beside me. At thirteen I spent two days sitting on a hospital bed as doctor after doctor filed into the room and took their turn listening to my heart. I had grown fond of my condition, to the prospect of open-heart surgery, the gravity of it, the nerve of it. I was devastated to learn, as the last doctor departed, that the "wait and see" had been successful. The murmur had diminished, it was tolerable, it had lost its drama. I would live.

My cholesterol is high. The sound is so commercial, so topical. I must push one step farther to see the profundity of it. It is a condition of the body, it threatens. It must be tended to. Like my thigh, it is something to accept, to live with. Now, it is clear, the "wait and see" is in the blood, it's the mortal thing. I will not grow out of it.

THE NOONDAY KARATE CLASS AT MY DOJO is a meager crew of middle-aged misfits. Their hips don't snap with the punch. The quick click of the *gi* that sounds clearly in the evening classes with twenty teenage kicks is silent at noon. I was verging on teardrops today as I struggled through to 1:30, failing among the noon losers. My back wouldn't support the leg lifts, there was no spark in my muscle through the blocks and the strikes. I was nervous and tentative. Last spring, before we were married, Ray and I went to night classes together. Now I go at noon more often than not. It's better with my schedule.

For four years in high school I swam. The decision was made during the summer of '76 when Nadia Comaneci was airborne in living rooms across America. I studied the players, every sport, and found only one that made use of women with my weight. I swam five miles a day for the next four years. When I cried from the frustration, the pain, it was in nine feet of water.

My instructor threw out the combination: head block, body strike, front snap kick. My mind has been training along with my body, my grasp of a sequence has quickened, until today. I floated, one step outside the movement. I defended, attacked, forgot. I moved my eyes slightly, tried to follow the class. The noonday class cannot be followed. I pulled air in through my mouth, over the lump in my throat, and watched the clock.

Ray is a racquet man. His body understands the physics of

having an extension on his arm. On our honeymoon, I swam sixty laps in the pool every day. He swung at endless tennis balls. Ray doesn't go to karate anymore. He doesn't like the feeling of condescension that comes with being taught alongside twenty teenagers. He goes to the club after work and lifts weight, plays racquetball.

When you swim, you are alone. You must push yourself to hit the wall. You have no means of language. You are totally free. I feel that sometimes, in the night classes, third back from the mirror, drenched by sweat, submerged in the power of the slick, black sixteen-year-olds from Haiti. Today, this noon, there were five of us. We all got a mirror, we all got a view.

The night classes are filled with fighters, they defend themselves against the world. At noon the battle is much closer.

AT TWO IN THE MORNING between Saturday and Sunday, Ray and I checked in at a Motel 6 just inside the Virginia line. We claimed our own full-size beds, reached out over the canyon between us, and kissed before settling into a free showing of *Thelma and Louise*.

I faxed the lab report of my blood test to my father this morning and wrote on the cover sheet that I was sorry to have missed his call yesterday but we had gone to Virginia, to see Suzanne get married. I imagine him receiving the fax, approaching the machine, ripping it off in pages as it transmits, reading the news that Suzanne is married. He looks up and out, shakes his head, thinks how long life can be and how short, and how smoothly the world spins.

The number on the scale went up this morning. Ray makes an effort to be out of the house before the weigh-in happens, but today he was only as far as the butter on his pancakes. I could see it in his eyes that he could see it in mine as I entered the kitchen before coffee. The problem is eternal, one diet for another, fighting with my body for twenty-three years. The last one blamed carbohydrates so I ate cheese and meat and eggs. Now we tiptoe around the words "highest coronary heart disease risk" as they read on my clinical laboratory report. I have been thin two and a half times in my life. Ray finished his pancakes and suggested we go out today, find a cholesterol-free diet book.

When I was seven, I ate twelve hundred calories a day, enough for a child. My mother took eight hundred, she drank her coffee black. My father made bets with the men at the club, large amounts of money wagered on the numbers from the scale.

My mother scolded me once after my friends went home. I would give them cookies when they arrived at my house. My mother saw it as a bribe, a tactic for bringing the games to my turf. I told her it wasn't true, that I would eat the cookies alone if necessary. In the kitchen of Carol Bacon's house, there was an entire closet filled, on seven shelves, with candy. She never wanted any of it. She preferred a single piece of individually wrapped cheese, which she would eat over the course of an entire episode of *Family Affair*. Carol wore Danskin that matched, shirts with horizontal lines that ran straight across her stomach and fell with ease over her waist.

The morning that fathers visited my second-grade class, I was dieting. We played a game with homonyms. We would stand, say the word, spell it, use it in a sentence, spell it another way, use another sentence, and so on, until the word was fully revealed. I introduced my father and Mrs. Rasmussen gave me my word, *waste*. There was a chuckle the moment the word was uttered, the quick leap to *waistline*. I spelled *waste* and said, "The wastebasket is big," then spelled *waist* and said, "So is my waistline." I patted my belly, took the laugh, and sat down, fully revealed.

I stood in front of the mirror today and searched for the new weight. For years I've pulled tight on the flesh of my arms,

flexed the muscles in my thighs. I've imagined Danskin drap-
ing, spandex resting.

Today there was the blood running, the heart pumping. This
is a full look at the body and a war against invaders. I feel out
of sorts, unfamiliar with the surroundings, home sick from
school, out of the loop, disconnected, removed; like a nap at
noon.

MY HUSBAND HAS BEGUN TO INSIST that he will quit smoking
when I quit smoking. He is not habitual. Since I've known
him, he has quit for long periods on three separate occasions.
I've never quit, never tried. I borrowed four vegetarian cook-
books today from Allen, my karate instructor, brought them
home, sat down at the kitchen table, lit a cigarette, and
thumbed through them.

Kate was living with a sculptor named David in 1984 when
I arrived at her door on East 4th Street with several grams of
cocaine. I was living on East 3rd with an Australian hair-
dresser named John. John introduced me to cocaine one flawless night in Los Angeles, where we were living in the Bel Air
garage of a Hollywood diva. We slept together in the garage
on a bed formed with matching couches pushed together. We
called it the crib. I sat in the crib cross-legged as John taught
me to snort. The man I loved—a bisexual, diagnosed psycho-
path named Freddie, who worked as the diva's personal assistant—leaned into my arm from the other side, purring like a
cat.

The cocaine I carried to Kate's house that night, the night
I would learn to smoke, was John's. He said, "Take it, have a
good time." We sat around a picture frame laid flat atop a
wooden crate filled with books. We slid the powder around
on the edge of a razor blade.

I do not remember specific cigarettes, only by genre: the one
at three in the morning as my last table struggled to pay their

bill, the one on the street after an interview, the one that makes the bus come, the one that follows a purchase, the first one of the day after the last swig of coffee with milk. I do not have to think anymore of Kate's meticulous lesson: the relaxed hand, the duration of the inhale, nose and mouth exhaling, blowing rings. I remember the one I'm having now.

I picked up my first cigarette several hours into that evening, lit it, sucked the smoke into my mouth, and exhaled with a laugh. As I practiced, Kate recounted her smoking-in-the-girls'-room days. I felt the dizzying cushion of smoking and we justified our way through most of John's cocaine.

I returned to 3rd Street early the next morning and handed the carefully folded slip of paper to John in silence. He took it without notice, felt the thinness, smiled, and said, "Ah, young girls and cocaine."

As I drove the Gowanus Expressway yesterday, I realized the way in which I will stop this smoking. First to go will be the ones I value most, alleviate the dread. I will finish my dinner with dessert, sit in bars and chew on straws, start the day with coffee. My last cigarette will be one I won't remember.

MY HUSBAND TELLS ME he has spent the few months since our honeymoon speaking only of sex to his analyst. Not so much with me, he says, but in him. I am jarred by his syntax, then comes the slow dawning. It is what he meant to say. I listen carefully as he speaks to me from his office, by phone. I fight the distractions, the work I must do. This is important. It is in him, apart from me.

I wonder sometimes why it had to be that I would meet my husband through Phillip, a fifty-year-old English writer whom I met many years before through a man named Andrew, Phillip's best friend from university and my first lover. It lightened my mystery, made life look too simple. It drew a line so clear, like direct descendants, as if ten years of living between Andrew and Ray never happened, as if I'd been handed off. The space between them is the rest of my life, the half that is only mine, the part I found myself. I am compelled to reclaim it.

I've been dreaming in halves, incompletes. Yesterday morning Vinny the cat woke me with his coughing. I jumped from bed, glad to be through the night. I had been made responsible for half a duck, a delicate wee creature who had no back end. He was my ward, my topic for an essay. He lived inside a tiny cardboard box fixed up like a pond with a glass door on one side.

We were friends, we made plans to fix him up, get him straightened away with a new back end like other ducks. But despite our deep regard for each other, he was compelled to escape whenever the door was unlocked. Only I could open it for conversation and care; I understood the timing involved, how to close it without injury or escape.

News of my duck spread and people gathered, chaos ensued. His door was opened, I screamed, flung forward to shut it in time, but was too late. He moved like lightning. I tried to clear the area, capture him before injury. He was so small, I could sense him only through motion, I listened for a rustle above the confusion of the crowd, moved in, and delicately cupped my hands around the movement. I stood slowly, opened my hands just slightly, hoping to find my duck unharmed. A moth sat in my palm. I had missed my chance, pulled off course. My duck was gone. I was envisioning him being crushed like a lost contact lens when Vinny coughed.

I'M FEELING THE RESTLESSNESS AGAIN, in our bed at night, but the watchful eye has shifted. We are no longer staring at each other. We drift off to sleep from within. I question how we might find our way back from another explosion; all the furniture has been stained, its wood cleaned to a glow. Only the old kitchen chairs with their green wood and wicker remain. Ray and I don't know about wicker, we're afraid of disintegration.

I met Andrew on a tree-lined street in a small midwestern town, a day after my seventeenth birthday. He sat folded into a wicker chair on a friend's front porch. I zoomed by on a skateboard, blond hair flying. As recently as the day before my wedding, he told me that this first vision of me remains carved into his memory. He says it was a stunning moment. Andrew still claims, on occasion, that he will never get over it. I was a girl sitting directly atop that cusp that spills out onto womanhood. I can spot it on the street, there is nearly a smell to it, the woman-child who doesn't see how carefully she is balanced. That is the beauty of it. The fall is in the comprehension. I fell almost a year later, on Andrew's arm.

Ray and I met in a Soho bar nearly ten years after that. He was at the wrenching end of a bad date and I was shadowing Phillip from bar to bar, as he charmed his way from one free beer to another. We entered Fanelli's Bar and Grill, and Ray says he remembers the moment. He says there was white light. My memory is not so generous like Ray's; I remember the meeting simply, fluorescent.

I thought I would marry Andrew. I lost my virginity to him. On my eighteenth birthday, he called from Oxford, where he was completing his Ph.D., and announced with optimism that I was finally half his age. My sophomore year of college we spent New Year's Eve together in a hotel room on Park Avenue. A year later we slept entwined on a fire escape overlooking the Holland Tunnel. My mother saw the way he looked at me once and said love like that does not happen twice. Years later she would recant, saying that I have led an extraordinary life. Days after my twenty-first birthday, Andrew married another woman. He felt compelled to commit, he said, seduced by the life around him, a profound need for security. We had never been in the same city for more than two days.

Several years more and Andrew would reappear in my life again, puzzled and empty, begging for absolution and a way out. I would take his hand and say that I could only give him one or the other. In the end, I would say he took neither. We never had a day to sit, to read a book or stare quietly into space. I remain in his life as the steadfast memory of delirious innocence. Resolution is a physical thing, it should come from the body.

Andrew still lives in my hometown in the American Midwest, with a wife who sharpens his ambivalence toward life and two daughters who destroy it. Phillip and Diane are our best friends. Ray is my husband. He is thirty-one years old and I am thirty. Three months ago we wed. This is our marriage. The "wait and see" is in the blood, the resolution in the body, for as long as it may last. This is all an act of faith.

TWO

Dead as a Doornail

TESTOSTERONE LEVELS ARE DECREASING in this country. Testicular cancer is on the rise. And, if you trust Barbara Walters, the culprit is estrogen. My dad told me all this when we were shopping for golf cart batteries this summer. Shopping for golf cart batteries and discussing my failed marriage—an expensive six-month joke that consisted of refinishing furniture and hurling my husband onto the floor whenever we tried to have sex.

I gave my father the concise version. "There was no romance, Dad."

Then the man behind the counter and my father started a discussion. It went like this:

"She won't hold a charge. I've had 'er hooked up since you left here this morning and she's still dead as a doornail."

"No point in giving it another try, I guess."

"Nah. If she were interested she'da been juiced up by now. Afraid you're outta luck."

"Well, what ya got?"

"Let me check for you."

Counterman disappeared and my dad and I started our own conversation . . . like this:

"Nice guy. Gave your stepmother a great price on a new set of tires. Treated her very well."

"That's nice...He calls his batteries 'she.' "

"So, what does that mean, 'no romance'?"

"We didn't have sex, Dad."

Counterman returned.

"Here you go. I think you'll be happy with this one. She's got a full guarantee. Any problems and they'll replace 'er, no questions. You know how to hook 'er up? She's opposite the one you brought in. Just have to be sure your cables are long enough to reach around. Here, let me show ya."

The men disappeared into talk of cables and posts. I walked out to the parking lot, leaned against my father's truck, and lit a cigarette. I leaned against a car and smoked like this on the day that Ray and I moved the final boxes out from our ex-home.

We stood in the middle of rooms that were bare but not quite. The many boxes that can be filled from empty rooms always astonishes me. This was the last of our stuff; a basket, two notebooks, Christmas ornaments, an extension cord.

Margaret appeared at the front door, looking sleepy. "Hey, you guys...Need help?"

I took a flower arrangement and went downstairs to smoke. I stared at the blossoms on the dogwood tree draped over the garage. Last summer, or the one before, I had a feeling I doubt I will ever feel again, the calm derived from knowing, accepting that whatever this is, it's fine enough.

Ray started the car and we pulled away from the driveway. Last times sneak up on me, always have. "The bird feeder," I said suddenly as I saw it hanging from the kitchen window.

"John will be happy to take it down," Ray replied, smiling as we both think how deeply the landlord disliked the unsightliness of it.

At the corner, our old corner, everything was growing; trees, flowers, colors emerging like a rushing tide. "I thought things would never bloom here again," I said as my eyes fell on a bed of tulips. I had no choice but to remember Valentine's Day when I looked at him with an ounce too much resentment and the entire house unraveled; curtains blew, dishes broke, cats ripped at upholstery. Flowers still wrapped in paper sat on the counter when I entered the kitchen that night. I saw them and turned. It hurt to look at them. We were not valentines anymore no matter how much we wished we were.

He put away groceries and when the counters were clear of absolutely everything else but the wrapped flowers, he lifted them and turned to me. I would have run from the room if I had followed my instinct, anything to avoid the moment of connection, the touch of our fingers if I reached out to take them.

He held out the flowers, hurting so badly and for so long that it now shone in permanence on his face. "Happy Valentine's Day," he said.

"Thanks," I said. "Tulips."

We turned from one another as I forced out words about their color and shape until I had nothing left to offer. I crushed them into a vase from our wedding day, toyed with their posture, and then stared at their cut stems, realizing that they were dying in perfect precision with us.

It's not a day for flowers, I thought, and turned to him, finally ready to talk.

My father appeared with his new battery, which he set carefully in the back of the truck, and said, "You're dealing with an entire generation of emasculated men. And I tell ya, I blame the goddamn feminists."

If estrogen is causing cancer in men, doesn't that suggest that we're bad for each other? And if testosterone levels are on the decline, doesn't that mean that the primal attraction must also be decreasing? And isn't it just possible that the charger wasn't giving the battery enough juice?

I said, "Well, Dad, the feminists aren't doing so well either."

THREE

Snow

I AM ALONE. IN THE NORTH, IN THE COLD. White ridges of ice and snow. My cats don't like it here, but I think they will adjust.

Desolate was all I could think during those last months before we headed north. In my stomach, my legs, my thigh. I was—I am—a cavity, surrounded by decay. Dangerous territory. I had to leave. The only burning ember, in my brain. Pure desire to finally be a single person, one and the same, no more voices.

I drove in my car through the puritanical mountains of the East, the slow roll-out to flat of the Midwest. And then north. Up toward deep glacial lakes and their peninsulas, but that only sat well for a short time. I crossed huge bodies of water and kept driving, looking for the house that my grandmother had lived in when she would leave for school on snowshoes, out the second-story window. Not enough. The cats were angry but we kept driving north, crossing great borders. I'm not looking for home anymore, just a place that fits. I've been driving so long that my left leg is numb, the damaged muscle now challenging the blood flow. I'm on foreign soil. The last conversation with people was days ago now.

I've left the car running so that the cats don't freeze. I am sitting on something meltable if the cold would ever stop. All around me, white ridges of ice and snow. Unless I'm looking for something white, everything will become apparent.

I DON'T HAVE A GOOD MEMORY. I remember everything. As the terrain loses its definition, as I begin to develop the concept that white has many colors; that memory is unfolding itself. I am watching the minutes in between the times of my life, detail by detail, I am educating me.

I am three; in pink, bright blond, peach-and-cream skin. I am eight; stretch shorts, thick ponytail, clenched fist. I am five; sailor swimsuit, arms in air, pouncing on waves. I am twenty; jogging on speed, muscle snap, damage. I am twelve; tight corduroys, frizzed curls, windup pitch. I am grown. Detail by detail, I will reconstruct myself. This time, for real.

WE ARE STILL DRIVING. I know I cannot stay outside forever. I must find shelter for my cats and for myself. Vinny, the black cat in the velveteen jacket with white accents, has found a way to squeeze onto the dashboard. This is so he can look directly into my eyes when he glares. I look past him, through the windshield, at the white.

THE CABIN APPEARED JUST AS WE NEEDED IT. Gas tank on empty. We have found a house on the ice. It is complete, as if left for a girl and her two cats. I am worried that when the spring comes we will find ourselves sinking in a lake that might be beneath us. Or it may be that ice just lives here; like sand or dirt or rock lives other places.

The glass in the windows, the wood of the walls; it is all secure. We're safe from the cold as long as we can find wood for the fire. I have seen brown and green not many days from here so I'm hoping that trees are behind the color. There is an ax outside the front door frozen just beneath the ice. I will chip away at it and we will be fine.

The cats stay buried in the yellow of the quilt on the bed. We are all tired but I stand poised at the window, rubbing my leg and watching, as pictures blow by.

IT IS THE COLDEST IT HAS BEEN. I am in bed for the third day but not because of the cold. I am exhausted. I know the promises I have made for the spring and the constant cold beats into me the knowledge that spring will come next. Time may be slow but it is constant and it is short.

I left the city in bright colors, the trees on vivid fire. I had information leading me to believe that I was missing something and more information leading me to believe that I would find what I was missing by traveling to the North. The wind told me. It whistled through my heart, making a mournful sound when it whipped around in the emptiness, screeching when it had to work its way around blockages and masses that have made themselves a part of me in recent years.

This is not rational. Rationale has deceived me before and I'm wary now of things making too much sense. When the wind spoke, I was confused just enough to listen.

Anatomy defines me. Beyond that, I'm lost. I am a made-up thing: part flowers, part work boots. My body shows signs of wear, years of discontent revealing itself in thick blood and broken muscles that cause pain and numbing. Love makes me angry and leaves me without hope. I cannot go home until I find out why.

I SAY OUT LOUD, "A BATH." It has been a long time since I've had a bath and it would be so nice to feel warmth seep into my bones, relax the muscles. I woke this morning and opened the door to the closet. Rung and hooks gone, there was a bathtub steaming, topped with bubbles, a towel draped perfectly. I am sure I am hallucinating but I strip and slide beneath the water anyway.

With the warmth comes feeling and I know, in that instant, that I am completely alone.

Vinny the cat spoke today. I asked him why he had taken so long if this is what he is capable of. He said he thought I needed the time to think things through. He has always thought so highly of me, he says, and he has always wished that I thought more highly of myself.

"It could have alleviated a lot of this travel," he says. Vinny is not a wanderer by nature. He is a cat who values home and hearth.

"I've made myself up, Vinny. I can't feel good about myself because I don't know who that person is. I lost her a long time ago."

"Everyone makes themselves up," he tells me.

"Not you."

"I'm a cat. I'm not so complicated." Then he thinks for a moment. "But I've probably made a little bit of me up too." He licks his paw and does a once-over on his right ear, then sits quiet, takes a breath, and speaks.

"I'm a cat. I know I've said that before but it bears repeating—I am a cat and a cat is a vicious, vicious beast."

"You mean, big cats—lions, jaguars," I say.

He goes after his right ear again, a little harder this time, as if he is disguising a vigorous shake of his head.

I continue, "You are a sweet being, Vinny. I think you're the kindest soul I have ever known."

He stops with his ear, stands. He steps with his front paws onto my thigh and then props himself up against my chest so that he stands erect and stares directly into my eyes.

"Did you know," he says in a low purr, "that it is in my mind sometimes to eat you."

We stare another moment into each other's eyes, he gives a single nod, steps down, and sits sphinxlike next to me. Together, we face the window in silence and time slips by.

I am still staring straight ahead when I speak again. "It's instinct, I guess."

"I guess, but you're so good to me that I can't believe it myself when the vision comes over my mind."

A fresh snow begins to fall as Vinny settles into a deep and curled sleep.

LATER, AFTER HIS NAP, I ask him if Sophie is also capable of speaking. He says she has little of value to say.

"But could she speak if she wanted to?" I ask.

He is quiet for a moment and then shakes his head.

"We must think of her as our cat, and that is not a bad thing."

Vinny's left ear pins back and he speaks to the window. "Sophie is a happy cat. Far happier than me."

"I," I say, "far happier than I."

"Whatever," he sighs, and leans away from me.

"I'm sorry." I want to scratch behind his ear but somehow now wonder if I have that right.

"Language is for communication. 'Me'—to my ear—denotes a deeper sense of melancholy and more profound sense of the history of sadness."

"That may be," I say, "but if everyone makes their own rules, then communication will break down. A misplaced comma can change an entire meaning."

"Did you understand, when I said 'me,' " he asks as he makes little quote marks in the air with his front paws, "that Sophie holds a lightness in her soul. An untouchable, angelic countenance that I will never touch, never know, because of an innate heaviness that has lived in my heart since my beginning?"

"Yes, I guess I did."

"All right then. Keep your commas where they belong," and he jumps onto the floor, disappearing around the corner of the kitchen door.

WHEN VINNY AND I FINISH DINNER TONIGHT, we sit quietly near the fire. My insides have been feeling particularly hollow in the last few days and I say so to Vinny.

"Why do you think that is?" he asks me, not taking his eyes from the fire.

"It's a loneliness, I think," I tell him.

"Lonelier than usual?" He seems a little surprised.

"I expect the worst in life," I say, sounding apparently scattered but feeling entirely linear. One does seem to lead to the other.

"When the phone doesn't ring," I continue, "it is because the love has stopped on the other end."

"We don't have a phone," he reminds me.

"I know. I'm talking about then. When we did. When we lived in the city. I was so certain every time. It wasn't a late train or an unexpected business call. It was the choice of the person on the other end to stop caring."

"Where did this come from?" he asks me, and now he looks at me with a certain degree of concern.

"It just struck me today." That is the truth. I was picking the ice away from the car. I felt strong and it was such an unfamiliar feeling.

"The absence of a phone has brought me some inner peace, Vinny."

"Well, that's fine, I guess. But I'm still concerned as to the origin of this line of thought," he says.

"Maybe I wish someone would be looking for us. But that's about as hopeless as trying not to notice that the phone isn't ringing."

"But usually the phone did ring, didn't it?" He is pointed in his question and he is right. Just as that last wave of pain—the one that would kill me—was beginning to form, there would be the earth-shattering crash, the ring. The adrenaline. The relief.

I turn to look at Vinny.

"There are tears falling down your cheeks," he tells me simply, passing the information along. I wipe them away and he shifts his weight to lean against my thigh. I adjust him slightly, away from the muscle that hurts me.

"I wish I expected more, Vinny."

"You're wishing for hope," he tells me. "That's like wishing for a wish."

My brow furrows and Vinny says, "Why waste time, just wish."

"That's very EST," I say.

"Whatever," he says, and shuts his eyes.

The fire cracks.

I FOUND VINNY STANDING ON THE WINDOWSILL TODAY, ears twitching viciously. He did not look at me when the floorboard squeaked beneath my step.

"What are you doing?" I ask him.

"Wishing for a visitor," he says forcefully, without turning, though he does sit back on his haunches with this statement.

"Why?" I ask, stunned by the coldness in his voice. He doesn't answer me so I ask him again, "Why?"

"You don't touch me anymore."

"Vinny . . . ?" I don't know what to say.

"You have very nice hands and I miss them." He takes a deep breath. "There. I've said it."

"Have I stopped touching you?"

"You know you have. Since the moment I spoke out loud," he answers, and I think I hear a crack in his voice, his throat tightening.

"You give a great belly rub," he says, and for the first time he turns to face me. His eyes are wide open and at their most beautiful green. "And how you knew just the right way to massage a cat's back, I'll never know. But it was wonderful, I'll tell you that, and I don't like my life without it."

I open my mouth, hoping that words will fall out but only a low raspy bit of air comes through.

"Don't you like me anymore?" he asks, and I hear the chink of my heart breaking.

"Vinny . . . I'm sorry." I am overcome with a sickeningly familiar feeling.

"You have problems with men, don't you?"

"Ummm . . . uhhh . . ." I am scared of falling from grace. I have always felt confident that my cats saw me as perfect and I'm sure that I'm on the verge of losing that.

"I've seen everything, you know, I've seen you stop touching before," he says.

I must have a reason, I think. I can't be incapable.

"I didn't want to disrespect you, Vinny," I finally say and walk farther into the room. "It's true that when you started to speak, I found myself uncertain of what was acceptable." I want to sit but can't quite make it to the couch.

"How is touching disrespectful?!" There is anger in his voice. "I really don't understand that!" His tail twitches for a moment and then lies still. "I'm a very smart cat but I suspect I would make a very ignorant human."

"Don't blame the humans, Vinny, I think it's just me. I have to think this through. I'm confused."

"Does the fact that I'm a boy cat bother you?" he asks.

"Well . . . but Vinny . . . you're—" He cuts me off.

"Don't say it. That's cruel. I am still a boy cat!"

"Yes, you are."

He walks his front paws out in front of him and stretches along the windowsill. As I watch him, the muscle in my thigh seizes and I suddenly gasp.

"What is it?" Vinny asks.

"Just my thigh. I'm fine," I say as I push my knuckles into the solid mass of mangled muscle and force it to stillness.

"Something is wrong with that leg," Vinny says.

"It's a damaged muscle. Nothing to be done."

"Come here."

I walk toward him upon his command.

"Sit," he says and I do, on the chair that leans against the wall between the door and the window. He extends his left front paw.

"Hold my paw," he says, "please."

I look at him, filled with guilt and shame, and he looks right back. I lift my left hand so that his paw falls into my palm and with my right hand, I softly stroke the white fur that makes him look like he's wearing spats. He closes his eyes and sighs.

"I'll try harder, Vinny, I promise," I whisper.

I look past him, out the window, and for the first time since we arrived here, I see something other than white. Far off in the distance, a green dot moves along the horizon and I know that Vinny's wish for a visitor will come true.

"Come into the kitchen," I say with a squeeze of his paw. "I'll fix you some milk."

He rises up on all fours and stretches. "Not milk, it really doesn't agree with me. Do we have any bouillon?" he asks. "I could really go for some beef bouillon."

"Let's see," I say, and stand as he jumps down and walks toward the kitchen. I look out the window and wonder how far is the horizon and how soon will Vinny's visitor arrive. I turn back toward the kitchen and Vinny is looking at me from across the room.

"Don't worry," he says, "we still have some days."

I HAVE STUDIED THE GREEN DOT and have decided that it is a truck. It's the jerkiness of its movement more than anything I

can actually see. It bounces along the horizon. Vinny won't
tell.

I ask him about the nature of his wish, whether it was for
him or for me. He will tell me nothing except that our guest
will do us all some good.

I broke through to the ax yesterday morning. It has taken
many weeks of constant picking to keep up with and finally
overtake the deep freeze that has held it prisoner. But I can't
use it because I can't leave. It's a two-day journey to the place
of color that might be trees and we have a visitor coming.

I expressed my concern about the firewood supply to Vinny
and he said that our visitor would bring all that we need.

This brings me to a standstill. The ax has been my center,
all things revolving around its release from the ice. Now it is
free and it is useless. I am left to schedule my days with no
middle. The pictures out my window are gone. Nothing has
blown by in days. I cannot will them into being. They come
on the jet stream and I see them only through a state of warm
serenity and I'm all frozen up.

EVERYONE IS SLEEPING BUT ME. I am openly envious of my
cats' affinity with sleep. They seem to have a higher understanding of the nature of comfort. They can turn anything into
a cloud and then rest perfectly upon it.

Now is an excellent time to sleep. It seems the only option
to waiting. With the dot moving so slowly along the horizon,
it seems as though we will be waiting forever. And I don't
even know for what.

Now I sit here, eyes open staring, but I don't see anything.
I try to imagine what I might wish for, what I might hope for
in the dot. I can't imagine what. I have food and clothes and
air and cats. I just want to survive. Anything more might raise
my expectations. Anything more might break my heart.

———

"SEX IS NOT PART OF ME. I keep it in a separate place," I say.

Vinny looks immediately uncomfortable with my sudden confession.

"Maybe this is something you should discuss with Sophie." He looks around. "Where is that cat?" he asks.

His panic makes me smile. My smile makes him flinch. He gets up, sniffs a random floorboard. He knows he's been revealed.

"Have you seen my pink-and-blue fuzzy ball?" he asks. "I feel like batting something around."

"I think it's under the couch."

His tail snaps.

"You'd think manufacturers would have figured that one out!"

Vinny is a little upset. I can tell by his ear twitch.

"I can't tell you how many of my things wind up under the couch. MAKE CAT TOYS THAT WON'T FIT UNDER A STANDARD COUCH! How hard could that be?! Do these legs look like they can reach three feet?! No!! Make cat toys size-appropriate!!! That's all any of us are asking!"

I move from my seat by the window and get down on all fours in order to help Vinny get his toys.

"Never mind," he says. "I don't feel like playing anymore."

"Come on, Vin. Here. I'll throw it and you can go get it. That'll be fun, won't it?" I throw his pink-and-blue fuzzy ball toward the kitchen. He watches it go, then hangs his head a bit.

"No," he says, and he walks toward the armchair. He stands with his head touching the dust ruffle. "I'll be in my office if you need me," and he disappears under the chair.

We are all anxious and the strain is revealing itself. I turn back to the window to check the progress of the green dot. It has disappeared.

———

VINNY PULLED SOPHIE OUT OF A DEEP SLEEP this evening by ramming his head alongside hers. I watched as she nuzzled him and fought to continue her slumber. Vinny would not stop.

"Let her sleep, Vinny," I say.

"I want her to dance," he says. "She hasn't danced in days and it will be good for us to see it."

"I didn't know she danced."

"Like an angel," says Vinny. He is washing her face now, preparing her for her performance. "It lifts my spirits to see her midair. Pardon me for saying so, but she moves like a bird. The very best there is of a bird captured in a cat. It's pure heaven. I'm surprised you've never seen it."

"So am I," I answer, stunned and glad to have a distraction from the gloom that has been settling around our feet.

"We're going to be cheered up," he says with great hope.

The gloom was born the moment the green dot disappeared. Though he won't admit it, I know Vinny doesn't understand what has happened either and he's concerned.

I turn back to the cats. "What was the dot, Vinny? Was it a truck? Is there someone out there who is lost now or hurt?"

Vinny is standing center in front of the fireplace. He clears his throat with a quick, gruff purr.

"And now, it is my deep pleasure to present the lyrical and ethereal...Miss Sophie."

And the dance begins. Miss Sophie moves on tiptoes, back arched. She looks shyly toward her audience as if she hopes no one will notice her in her shiny orange coat alone on a vast stage, bathed in a crackling fire spotlight.

"She has a keen perception of the importance of under-statement," whispers Vinny without taking his eyes off her. "Watch this next movement."

And with that she stretches her front legs forward and shifts back with her weight so that her tail and little orange butt reach upward while her head and front haunches spread along the floor. Her mouth opens wide.

I lean into Vinny. "She's stretching and yawning, right?"

Vinny stiffens, refusing to look at me.

"It is the mute scream of the instinctual beast." There is a definite contempt in his tone.

I fall back into the couch, having decided to be mute myself. That's when Sophie springs from the floor, all fours all at once, and I am transfixed. Vinny was right. She is a soaring bird, she is a playful otter, she is the grace in a gazelle. Her movements are eclectic; full body spins and bends, then contortions as she nearly folds over on herself. Then come the screams and howls, joy and pain laid across the passion of her dance. Back and forth she goes, from windswept to jagged edge. Then, just as I begin to think her passion has brought on some sort of seizure, she pulls herself up, balances on back legs, and reaches high up into the air, so delicate as if she is reaching out of herself to touch the tip of a light beam. She comes down from her tiptoes and rolls full body into the floor. She curls nose tip to tail, contracting all the while, until her face is buried in paws and then she is asleep.

Vinny and I sit without breathing as we let silence take its turn.

I finally turn to Vinny to gauge his reaction. "It's sort of Isadora Duncan meets Mummenschanz," I say.

Vinny's eyes are closed, his head held high, swaying. He is lost in the moment. I put a gentle hand on his little shoulders and fix my gaze on the fire. But from the corner of my eye, I see his white spat paw rise up as if to wash his face. He makes a quick swipe across his right cheek and I wonder quietly if a cat's tears are salty.

WE'RE CLEANING THE KITCHEN WHEN VINNY ASKS, "Do you miss TV?"

"I miss *Roseanne*."

"Yeah, I miss *Roseanne* too..." He continues to lick the stubborn baked-on cheese from last night's casserole off the stove.

He hardly stops licking long enough to add, "And *The Joy of Painting*."

I look at him with a question.

"PBS. The guy can paint an entire oil landscape in a matter of minutes. I find it fascinating."

"Is it true that cats paint?" I ask him, remembering a very strange book I read once on the subject.

"Not with that kind of speed," he says, shaking his head in admiring wonder.

My sweeping is being delayed by Miss Sophie. I was reprimanded when I asked her to move. She is choreographing a new piece, I am told, which has its roots in the nature of tile. She can only work in the kitchen.

"I guess I'll finish this later...when Dame Sophie takes a break."

"I'll let you know," says Vinny.

My mind is on the green dot. It has been several days now and it has not reappeared. The wood supply is dangerously low and I know that I am going to have to make the journey to the color that might be trees very soon or we will be in some real trouble. I am about to leave the kitchen to check the horizon again when Vinny's head jerks up.

"And Ted Koppel!" he states. "I miss Ted."

I WOKE WITH A JOLT THIS MORNING, so early that the sun was just barely licking the sky. My eye on the horizon, nothing. Only white and wind. The wind so strong that I could see it though there is nothing to be blown—except the green dot. I think for a moment that the earth is flat and that the green dot has been blown over the edge, then I remember Columbus.

Then I remember my dream, a dream in which I am still married.

I am in the house where we lived. I am dressed for a jog. I am anxious. I don't know why I'm afraid but I suspect that I might not really be there. Although I know that I am not anywhere else either. Then I come to understand that I might just be dead even though my body is still up and around. With this understanding comes the revelation that my body, though still functioning at task level, will no longer replenish itself. I must be particularly careful of scrapes and gouges as they will not heal. My thigh is of particular concern.

I am at the kitchen table, making reservations on a train, calling myself Euphenia Graham. I am counting the money I have collected in small bills and coins. I hold a quarter in my hand and when I set it down, there is a black circle in my palm. More evidence that I am dead, carbonized.

Then I am making the bed. Adrenaline pumping as I calculate the exact moment when it will be obvious that I am making the bed. I suspect outlaws are prowling about and may take me away at gunpoint. I am desperate to leave evidence for my husband and the police, that they know the abduction happened as I was making the bed.

Then I am taking the video camera out of the closet. It has a note taped on it that says: "Honey, please watch the video." I plug the camera into the TV, check the framing of the shot, and, using the remote control, I begin to record. I say, "It is January fifth, 11:35 A.M. I am leaving now to run counterclockwise around the park. If you are watching this, it means I'm missing. I never returned home." Then I turn slowly in order to show all my angles, more evidence for an accurate and ample description. I stop recording. I am opening the front door of the apartment when I wake up.

DRIFTING OUT AMONG THE SNOWCAPS, thoughts of home and summer and childhood birthday cakes.

"What are you doing?" Pouncing paws landing in my lap.

"WHAT?!" I shout, startled to my core. Vinny is standing on me, looking in my face.

"You scared me, Vinny!" I say, trying to catch my breath.

"You've been sitting here for hours. What are you doing?"

My hand on my chest, adrenaline just starting to fade. "Don't do that again. OK?"

"You cannot will the dot into being," he says to me.

"Look," I say, "you're the one who made it appear in the first place. Tell me what you know and maybe I'll be able to relax about it."

"What could I know? I don't know what it is," he says with deep sincerity.

"Well, you were the one who was wishing for a visitor. Who were you wishing for?"

"If I tell you, it won't come true. Don't humans teach their children anything?" He is honestly disturbed.

"Right," I say, disturbed in my own right.

"There is no point in worrying about it," he tells me. "It's out of your jurisdiction."

He looks at me, waiting for me to agree. Eventually I nod.

"Listen," he says, obviously changing the subject, "did you pack my comb?"

"I think so."

"I could really use a once-over if you've got the time. It's very dry up here and my dandruff is getting a little out of control."

"You do have a problem with that, don't you?" I say as I give him a tap to jump down so that I can get up.

Walking to the closet to check my bags, Vinny is on my heels. "Well, you don't have to be rude about it," he says. "I'm sure you have dandruff too but you blonds and orange things don't show it!" This is clearly a weak spot. I decide not to push it.

"I would love to give you a comb, Vinny," I state. I rummage around in the closet while Vinny sits patiently at the door.

"You know," he says, "I would gladly do it myself if I had thumbs."

I smile.

"Sure. Funny to you," he continues, "you have them. Tape them down some time. See how much you can get done!"

"Here it is," I say as I shove everything back into the dark closet, closing the door on the chaos. "Let's sit by the fire."

On the couch, I nestle myself into a corner. Vinny leaps up and arranges himself for my combing convenience. I start at the nape of his neck and pull the comb down all the way through his tail. His purr kicks in like an engine.

"Boy oh boy, that's a fine feeling," he murmurs.

His coat ripples as his legs extend outward beyond his control, stretching almost past their point. His eyes are slammed shut and his purr has taken on a chortling quality.

"Feels good, huh, Vin?" I say, but he doesn't speak, only rumbles through his purr.

After a few more strokes, Vinny lifts his heavy lids. Like a doper just moments beyond the nod, he is back on the planet but barely.

"You know," he slurs, "I wrote a poem about it once."

I try not to laugh. He hates being laughed at. He's drunk on combing.

"What are you talking about, Vinny?"

"Thumbs," he says, "I wrote a poem about thumbs."

"Can you recite it?" I ask him, anxious to hear it.

"Oooohhhhh," he says as he pushes his back legs against me to reposition himself, "this was years ago...I don't know..."

His legs are now sticking straight up in the air, his enormous belly fully revealed. I set the comb aside and proceed to execute the belly rub. His head falls back, his legs splayed; from this position, he speaks.

" 'Ode to a Fifth Digit,' " he exclaims, "by Vincent the Black Cat."

Beneath my hand, I feel him take a deep breath, he begins.

Oh what a wondrous thing it would be
to have an opposable thumb.
I would clamp, I would grip, I would grasp,
  I would squeeze,
I would be more selective with crumbs.

Imagine the glory of holding with grace
an object whose surface is shiny.
I would dance with it delicately held in my paws
from here to the hills of Killarney.

But these are mere dreams of a jaguar midget.
I am only a cat, I have no fifth digit.

Vinny lets out a sigh. I lift him from my lap and hold him close.

VINNY BAKES BREAD. It's a good project for a boy with no thumbs, though measuring is still a problem. There is flour absolutely everywhere and there is an enormous amount of orange and black fur in the dough itself. I point this out to Vinny but he says that they will enjoy it anyway so I continue to assist them however I can.

"The fur just comes out," he says, "we haven't any choice."

Vinny and Sophie take turns kneading. By my standard, the dough is more than ready to rise but they can't seem to stop. They are, after all, excellent kneaders and seem to find the work very gratifying. We have nothing but time as we wait for the visitor to reappear so I let the afternoon slip by.

It is nearly dark when I ask Vinny how much more kneading he anticipates.

"I suppose it's ready," he concedes, and signals a tired but satisfied Sophie to pull out.

"Vinny?" I say. "Tell me the story of your life."

"What?" He's a little confused. "But you've been there every step of the way...well...except...except for...the beginning..."

I have always wondered how bad it was in the beginning. He was a terrified little kitten and though I would never say so to his face, still maintains some neurotic tendencies.

"I want to know the beginning," I say, "and I want to hear your interpretation of your life story even if I was there. Tell it to me as if we've just met."

"The whole thing?" He seems a little overwhelmed.

Sophie has extricated herself from the bread dough and has settled atop the open bag of flour. She seems ready for the telling of a tale.

"You better make some cocoa," says Vinny, "and for me, a little ginseng tea."

I set about preparing the tea as Vinny uses his mouth and full body weight to tip the bread pan onto its side. He gets behind the furry dough and rolls it into the pan. I take the pan and put it in the oven.

"It's Chia bread," I say, which passes without appreciation.

"Just this life, right?" he says.

"What are you talking about, Vinny?"

"You just want this life's story. That's what you're asking, right?" He is standing on the counter awaiting instruction.

"Do you believe in past lives?" I ask.

"What are you asking? Do I know my past lives or do I believe them?"

"What?" I'm baffled at his response as I set three teacups on the counter.

"Well, for example, I know I was Napoléon Bonaparte but I can hardly believe it." He is staring at me, waiting for the clarification of my question. I stare back in disbelief.

"Just this life," I finally say, "but I'd like to come back to your other lives a little later."

"That's fine. But it's a long story."

"I would imagine," I say.

He settles himself into a kitty meat loaf, all feet tucked in and out of sight.

"Well," he says, "where to begin? I was born in a litter, the living mixed in with the dead."

Sophie and I both gasp.

"There was a nip in the air but buried in my mother's fur, I barely noticed it. My two dead brothers and one dead sister stayed with us for a time as my mother tried to coax a life back into them. We were happy to keep them as we'd grown accustomed to their shapes, but eventually it became clear that they would not be with us much longer. One day I awoke and there only remained me and my two sisters. I never heard another word about the others."

"Did they get eaten?" I ask, immediately regretting the question.

Vinny looks at me, a dull ache in his eyes. "I just said I don't know."

"Sorry," I mutter, "keep going."

Vinny takes a breath. "My mother was a saint. Not in this life, of course. In this life, she was a cat. But I remember her from before and she was a saint."

I nod.

"I can tell you that we lived under a bush near a brick building corner, but beyond that I'm unsure as we were never allowed to wander away. It was dangerous, my mother told us. There were cars and worms and humans . . . glass and fleas and hard rain. It was no place for kittens of hers, she would say. We were to stay in the bush until we were older and stronger and she would bring us whatever we needed until then."

Sophie is wide eyed and nodding her head in agreement. She seems to understand the dangers.

"Well," continues Vinny, "as I'm sure you've guessed, one day my mother did not return home."

I take a breath, about to ask a question, but am silenced with one look from the storyteller.

"I don't know what happened to her. There were rumors. I heard them all. A car. A psychotic tom. I even heard she was captured and sold into the fur slavery market. It doesn't really matter. The point is we were left alone, having never ventured beyond the bush, and it was my duty as the boy to take the lead."

"That's chauvinistic," I say.

"It is not chauvinistic. My body was bigger and had testosterone." Vinny looks directly at me and says again, "Had."

"OK, OK," I say, "so you took the lead because you were bigger, not because you were the boy."

"Boys generally have bigger bodies. It just makes sense to have boys in charge of physical protection. I wasn't in charge of strategy. That was my sister's job. Her head was bigger and had more brains in it, so she formulated the game plan."

"There were two sisters, weren't there?" I ask.

"It was Gray who had the big head. She was very smart. I learned how to think from her."

"And the other one," I ask.

Vinny's head drops just slightly and he seems unable to continue for a moment. Then he says with eyes nearly shut, "She was orange."

Sophie, whose head is dropped to her paws in a slow fall into sleep, opens her eyes and lifts her chin just slightly, a soft mew escaping.

"We lost her," continues Vinny. "She was small and weak

but I tell you, such a soul . . ."—he slows in his speech—"is a rare thing."

He steals a glance at me as he softly waves his tail in the air and lets it dip down to brush Sophie's cheek. I am afraid to speak so he continues.

"I believe in my heart that she died. There was nothing to her, she could not have survived alone. But all I can tell you for certain is that I turned around and she was gone. We were moving from shadow to shadow, looking for food. Gray had told her if she ever felt afraid, to stand in a shadow, not to move, and we would find her. But we never did."

Vinny stops speaking and we sit silent.

"You did the best you could, Vinny."

"That's what I tell myself," he says, and then looks at his cup. "Is there more tea?"

I put the kettle back on the fire and wait for Vinny's tale to continue. Sophie and I mark time as he takes a moment to gather himself.

"I'll tell you," he says, "I am not the same cat I was then. I have not been the same cat since the moment Little Orange vanished. Before that I was really quite something."

He shakes his head from side to side and lets out a chunk of air, which I have come to recognize as something akin to a chuckle.

"Cocky? You never saw such a strut," he says. "I was God's gift to cats . . . but when I turned around and saw only slashes of light and empty shadows . . . when I lost Little Orange . . . my perception of the world and the way that I sat on it . . . changed. It became what it is now, a true perception of the lasting tragedy and constant triumph of merely surviving."

The three of us have each fallen into our own slow nod of the head. Though when I look more carefully upon Sophie, I see that she is actually deep in sleep and her nod is simply the rhythm of her purr.

"With that," says Vinny suddenly, "came fear and anxiety. I was filled with doubt. I could no longer take the lead."

"It's understandable that you would be shaken," I say quietly.

"I was not shaken. I was changed." He pauses before going on. "But that's what we do in this life, isn't it? We change. We find ourselves slowly and in little bits."

I nod to him, trying to grasp his full meaning.

"So, where was I?" he asks, dipping his tongue to his tea and purring just a bit as the stuff slides down his throat.

"Of course. So it was Gray and me. Gray was subtle about it but she took control of things after that because she knew I no longer could. And with her at the helm, we muddled through, into the time of deep snow—not a particularly good season for either of us, her in gray and me mostly black. But we got through to the season of dead trees and lights . . . your Christmas," he says, tossing his head in my direction.

"Odd thing, your killing all those trees," he says.

"Yeah, I know. It's a pagan ritual."

Vinny lights up. "Pagan ritual?! I'll give you pagan ritual! Have I got a story for you. It was deep in the Black Forest. Ninth century . . . no, tenth—"

"You're digressing, Vinny," I say, not quite ready for his past lives yet.

"Ah, so I am," and he clears his throat. "It was just after the New Year . . ."—he looks at me with a brow raised, making clear his disapproval of that holiday as well—"an ordinary day; cold, clear. I was captured."

He stops and I look at him expecting more.

"It's that simple really. They got me from behind. Never saw it coming. Cold, clear day, then dark brown burlap. Boom. Changed again."

"What about Gray?" I ask.

"I hope she saw it happen," he says, and the dull ache

returns to his eyes. "I hope it wasn't like Little Orange all over again. I don't know that she could have survived another un-answered question. I screamed so maybe she heard that. But I could tell I was being moved quickly. I don't know that I was near enough to her for her to hear..." He trails off.

"In any case, this began my days and nights in the asylum, surrounded by half-mad cats like me. At first I held a hope that my mother or Little Orange might step from the deafening crowd, but I soon realized that that was foolish thinking. They were gone.

"I kept to myself. It was at the asylum that I first developed my taste for underbed living. There was a corner spot, beneath the bed, farthest away from open space, that I claimed as my own—"

"That's where you were when I found you," I exclaim.

"That's right. That's where I was for many, many days. There was a relief to it all, I'll admit. Away from the dangers of the street. But it was a sad place. Dark and stale. Hope was hard to carry there."

"She was a crazy old lady, that one who lived there," I say.

"She did the best she could with what she had," he responds. "She did what she felt she must."

"Do you wish you were never caught?" I ask him.

He thinks for quite a while, then, "If I had kept Little Orange from harm's way, I would have lived like a king on the streets forever. I was just that kind of cat. But as it was, I would not have lasted. I needed to be caught." He goes silent again.

"But I do miss some things," he says.

"Like what?"

His lipless mouth purses a bit and he seems hard put to look me in the eye.

"I miss peeing out-of-doors," he utters.

I bite the inside of my cheek.

"Exhilarating sensation, especially when a cool breeze blows..." He hesitates but I can tell there's more he'd like to say.

"What?" I ask.

He clears his throat. "That's why I pee on the rug in the bathroom sometimes, which I am sorry about because I know it annoys you... but when that ceiling fan is whirring and the moist shag of the throw rug is nestled between my toes... sometimes I can close my eyes and be back under the bush... my mother, Little Orange, Gray, and the dead ones... all around me... and I just can't help but relieve myself and feel that combination of steaming heat and gentle breeze."

His eyes are closed and I know that he has finished for now.

"You can start up at the point where we meet tomorrow," I say.

"If you wish," he responds, and he nestles himself into a curled sleep.

I lift his teacup slowly and kiss him lightly on his head.

WE AWOKE TO A RAGING BLIZZARD THIS MORNING. I was rising into consciousness, feeling the cats work their ways up the bed. They sleep under the covers, about knee level.

Vinny's head pops out from underneath the quilt, he turns toward the window and says, "Good Lord!"

I focus my eyes and follow his gaze. Ripped fragments of white whip around outside the window in a crazy chaos. A high scream pierces the air as the wind slices through the snow.

Sophie appears from beneath the quilt, her eyes only half open, then she bolts into the day. She moves quickly to the edge of the bed, ready for breakfast and a good stretch, then stops as her eyes stick on the window. She hunkers down and extends her neck. She drops to the floor. Slinking across the ground, she stops in her tracks on several occasions, looks from side to side, and then continues forward, toward her prey. She slides up the chair that sits near the window, then rises upward slowly. Her paw lifts a few inches up and then, *wap . . . wap, wap.* We all sit paralyzed.

Sophie extends upward to survey the damage, stares hard, then spins around and hightails it back to the bed.

She is under the covers and nestled against my belly before Vinny is able to say, "Seems like a good day to stay in bed."

"I'm going to have to go for wood, Vinny," I say.

"You cannot go today. It's as good as snapping your own neck," he says.

"But I can prepare today."

I work my way out from under the covers. Vinny lets out a grunt of disapproval.

"The dot is gone, Vinny," I say. "We can't just wait on indefinitely. We're running out of wood."

He seems to concede my point.

"I will pack and prepare for my journey and you will continue with the story of your life."

I hang my legs over the side of the bed and my left thigh shoots a painful spike down the length of my leg. It reminds me of what I know.

On some level, I know that the doctor who told me my leg contained an irreparable ruptured hamstring was wrong. On some level, I know that there is no damaged muscle there at all. On some level, I know that my thigh has been a storehouse for misinformation and discord, years and years of it, and it is reaching critical mass. It is a growing thing in my thigh, a strange kind of organic that is working its way round to deadly and it needs to be excised. It is the keeper of my flame and the breath to blow it out.

On some level, I know that I am in for it.

———

"It was a Tuesday," says Vinny from high atop his mound of pillows. He has nestled in to unfold the rest of his story and I am gathering supplies, trying hard to pack enough without becoming too much. Sophie is listening as she absentmindedly repeats movements over and over, obviously securing choreography into her muscle memory.

"Late in the day, if I'm not mistaken. The room was dark the first time I heard your voice," he says to me.

"You hid from me," I tell him.

"I did not hide. I simply did not make myself seen."

"Were you afraid of me?" I ask.

"It was not a question of fear. My spirit was broken. I was not in my right mind. All I could know was myself so I kept separate and alone so as not to confuse the world or be confused by it." He stops talking, then adds as a matter of fact, "I did not fight you when you reached for me."

"Yeah...well, it took me half an hour to maneuver myself far enough under the bed...you didn't need to fight..."

"But I could have. Though it was not the cat that I was, to fight. No. I simply pulled back as far as I could, until jailed by a corner of walls. Then I waited, for my options to run out, for my only choice to be labeled 'not enough,' for an arm that would reach out farther than I could pull back. And there you were, at the end of that arm."

"What did you think of me the first time you saw me?" I ask him.

Vinny pins his ears back, his eyes close to a squint. Suddenly Sophie catapults up into the air, spins in midair, and lands crouched, her skinny orange legs like coiled springs.

"What the hell is that, Vinny?" I ask. "Why does she do that out of the blue? What's happening in her brain?"

"She almost got stepped on by the pig," he says.

"What?!"

"There's a pigpen that extends into that part of the living

room—sometimes I completely forget that you don't see other dimensions," he says as a point of fact.

I find myself looking warily around the room.

"There are layers and layers of existence here," he continues.

I am rubbing my face with my hands. "Where's the pig now?" I ask him.

He glances toward the fireplace and nods in the direction of the far corner. "There."

I am squinting my eyes, pressing my palms against my temples.

"Nothing to worry about," says Vinny. He chuckles a little. "We don't get in each other's way but Sophie forgets that sometimes. I suspect it's her choreography. She becomes so entranced that she easily startles. Quite frankly, the pig could step directly on her and not a hair would be ruffled. So," he says, changing his tone, "what did I think of you...?"

I have returned to my packing but find that I am thinking twice about my every move, wondering who I might be touching and in what dimension.

"I felt an immediate confidence," Vinny says.

"Really? You seemed so terrified," I tell him.

"I felt confident that you were a fine choice. That doesn't mean I wasn't filled with dread about facing the world as a whole, which was what I was about to do. I didn't care for the man with you." Vinny stops. "Do you know I can't even remember his name."

"Yeah. Neither can I. Let's just fast-forward to when it was just us."

I am suddenly aware that I do not want Vinny to give me his views on absolutely everything he has witnessed in my life.

"I've made some pretty stupid moves, Vin," I say.

"Not to worry," he answers, "they happen in every life. I've never gotten through a single one without more than my share of embarrassments. But you have to forgive yourself. Otherwise you might as well wrap yourself in burlap and throw yourself into the river," he says, shaking his head from side to side, an odd confirmation of truth that eventually lulls him to sleep.

AFTER HIS NAP IT TAKES A LITTLE CAJOLING on my part, but Vinny agrees to continue his story.

"So there I was, a cat with a home," he states, always good with his openings.

"I understood my responsibility to find my place within it, but that was complicated by the presence of the gray one . . ." Vinny pauses for a moment, then says, "Taxi, may he rest in peace."

"You didn't get on with Taxi right away, did you?"

"He had control issues, not uncommon in gray ones," confirms Vinny, then adds, "With my sister being a rare exception."

He hesitates before saying any more. Then, "But I loved him like a brother and was crushed when we lost him . . . such a painful death . . . It's a horrifying disease, that feline leukemia . . ."

He looks at me. "You know I tried to find a way to let you know he wasn't well . . . that this was no fur ball . . . but he went so quickly . . ."

"How come you didn't get sick, Vinny? I mean, it's a very contagious disease."

"Physical health is an emotional state of mind," he answers.

"What are you saying? You willed yourself into staying healthy?" I ask him.

"Simply put, I suppose so. I am a longtime student of mind-body medicine." He glances over at me and I get the sense that he is gauging my reaction. I remain serious and nod slowly so that he will continue.

"I'm happy to talk with you about it, but it's not something I wish to gloss over lightly—a quick explanation pushes it too easily into the realm of pop psychology and I find that very annoying."

"I see," I say. "Did you try to talk to Taxi about it . . . when he was sick . . . ?"

"Taxi never put much stock in me or my ideas . . . I mean no offense by this, but he was not a particularly friendly or enlightened fellow . . ." Vinny seems uncomfortable but continues, "I don't know if you were ever aware of his views . . . very conservative . . . from what I have gathered from my years on top of the TV, listening to Ted Koppel and what have you . . . Well, I think you might have considered Taxi to be . . . well . . . very Republican."

"Really?" I am a little stunned by this. "I will say, you did seem to blossom after he was gone."

"Well, the whole climate changed, don't you think?"

"I suppose so . . . but I did love him . . . Republican or not," I say.

"As I said," immediate in his response, "I loved him like a brother."

We both take a moment for silence as Taxi and his memory permeate the room.

"Am I the only one who wants lunch around here?" Vinny suddenly asks, and without further ado, he hops down off the bed and takes himself into the kitchen.

I AM FINISHING MY TUNA FISH by wiping my finger along the bottom of the bowl, getting every last bit. I am aware now of how much energy I am about to need. Scared at the prospect of gaining firsthand knowledge of what it might be to "drop in my tracks."

We have had a quiet lunch and my thoughts have taken me out of the cabin. I am in a fog as I watch Vinny calmly move from his lunch to Sophie's and her, unquestioningly, stepping back.

"Hey!" I snap.

Sophie looks at me with wide butterscotch eyes. Vinny does not flinch.

"Vinny?!" I snap again.

He looks up, irritated at being interrupted.

"What?!" he snaps back. "I'm trying to eat, please."

"That's not yours. You ate yours already."

Sophie looks at Vinny, a bit nervous at the confrontation, but I think I detect a hint of pleasure in her face. Vinny, however, looks at me as if I am speaking French.

"That's Sophie's. Why are you eating her food?"

"Because I am done with mine," he states simply.

I let out an indignant grunt and shake my head.

"It really isn't your concern, lady, this is between Sophie and me." His tone is remarkably condescending.

"But it isn't fair. She wasn't done."

"This is our agreement. Why is it suddenly a problem for you?"

"Because it's not right, Vinny. You should take care of her. You're the older and the wiser."

"I'm also the bigger," he says, and he laps up the last chunk of food, Sophie looking on in complete acceptance.

"I thought you were evolved, Vinny," I say, trying to sting him with a final blow.

"I am evolved. One has nothing to do with the other. It's just the way it is...law of the jungle."

He is waddling toward the door to the living room, his stuffed belly throwing off his gait.

"It's piggy, Vinny," I state.

"Oink," he says, not looking back at me, and then he is gone, to a quiet lie-down near the fire.

I am left with Sophie, who is looking at me, head tilted to one side.

"You shouldn't let him do that, Sophie," I tell her, and with that she arches her back, stretches, and exits the kitchen in search of Vinny.

I am putting the dishes in the sink, choking on futility, "law of the jungle" ringing in my ears.

VINNY AND I HAVE LET OUR ARGUMENT settle into a silent battle. Nothing has been said for an hour. He pretends to sleep, his head held high, eyes shut. Sophie is dancing with the curtain.

To break the silence, I push a can of string beans off the edge of the table, creating a deafening crash up against the expanse of quiet. Everyone jumps. Vinny is so startled his skin ripples for several seconds.

I smile guiltily. "Sorry," I say.

"Hmmph," says Vinny.

"Are you going to continue your story?"

"What's to tell?" he asks flatly. "It's just a series of meals, mine and whoever else's I can steal." He has clearly been stung.

I feel rotten, filled with remorse for spiking his evolution. I pick up the canned vegetables and set them on the table. I can't look him in the eye.

"I'm sorry," I say.

"Me too," says Vinny. "It's tough though, it's an instinctual response."

I nod, trying to let it lie though I want desperately to fight for Sophie's dish rights. Vinny sighs quietly and I see relief wash across his face. He straightens his posture and I know he is gearing up for another round of storytelling. Then he starts to shake his head slowly.

"What?" I ask him.

"We've lived with a great many men," he says, and he stares at me, waiting for a response. I stare back.

"Nesting—it's an instinctual response," I say, animal to animal.

Vinny doesn't waste breath on responding, but simply stares at me, animal to animal, waiting for truth to surface.

"I don't know, Vinny. I played out the same scenario over and over."

"Why? What have you been trying to prove?"

"Prove?"

"I think so, don't you?" Vinny is very direct, calm, and well groomed.

"Well...I can give you my intellectual analysis about commitment and the permeation of society's rules into each and every psyche," I say.

"No, please don't," he says. "I've heard you explain that one to all of your closest friends and, quite honestly, it's never rung particularly true to me."

Vinny has flipped himself over on his back. He is slowly stretching his various legs up into the air. This makes his eyes droop. He battles a yawn.

I have taken the snowshoes out of the closet and am oiling the wood and leather, hoping they are not so dry that they will leave me stranded. Sophie, sitting up, has fallen asleep, her head is working its way toward the floor.

Vinny stops his stretch and rolls his head around so that he looks me in the eye from an upside-down point of view. He gives it a beat and then asks, "Why did we get married?"

We are stuck in this stare-down. I don't know how to answer him. Finally I say, "I gave up...lost hope."

"How could such a sad thing happen," he asks me, heartbreak all around him, "in a world with so much music and dance?"

Without warning, there are tears in my eyes. "You are asking me questions that I don't have answers for, Vinny. I don't know."

His paws, all four, are stretched out completely. "Maybe they are not answers to know but to feel," he says, and with that he unexpectedly falls onto his side with a thud.

"Uugh...oh, lady, I'm getting old," he sighs. "There was a time I could lie like that for hours..."

I lean the snowshoe against the table and sit on the bed next to Vinny. His head in my lap, my tears flow steadily.

"What I feel is that I don't know how to be a girl," I say, not sure what I mean. Vinny makes no move toward a response and I understand that he is now just going to listen.

Sophie has come awake, caught a glimpse of the snowshoe, and pulled herself into a slither. She is stalking a beast. Vinny and I watch her as she creeps across the floor. Inches from the snowshoe, she stops, then noses forward, jumps back.

Vinny shakes his head, closes his eyes, then says, "Look up *cat* in the dictionary, you'll see a picture of her."

Sophie is warily extending her front paw. She touches the shoe, jumps back. I know this will continue for a good long while and find its predictability a comfort.

VINNY HAS OPENED HIS EYES and is looking up at me from his niche in my lap.

"You were saying?" he says.

I take a breath. "I have watched girls all my life. Not all girls...just those girls who really know they're girls. They know something I don't. Want things I don't."

"Is this a problem?"

"Only if you want to fit in," I state. "Those are the girls who get the rewards...the loving smiles and kind nods."

I fall silent for a moment, stroke Vinny's finely formed head.

"There are fewer and fewer of those girls, by the way," I say. "At least, I don't see as many as I used to."

"Every species evolves," says Vinny. "There was a time when three-quarters of the cats I knew were polydactyl...not anymore..."

I nod.

"Anyway," I continue, "my sense of girlhood has definitely been acquired. There is nothing in me that has ever burst forth unsummoned that reeks of girliness."

Vinny does not respond, having returned to his role as the silent listener. So we sit in silence. He looks up at me, waiting. Annoyed at my need for a constant prompt, he twitches his tail three times and then finally blurts out, "And that matters because...?"

"You just asked me about the many men we've lived with. I believe these things are related...but never mind about this. You"—and I point at the velveteen boy—"are supposed to be telling me the story of your life. I have packing to do."

With that I stand abruptly, sending Vinny flailing in a roll onto his side, victim to his big belly, an awkward moment. He struggles, recovers, and looks at me with great disdain, fully annoyed.

"Fair warning is all I ask...," he says with a glare and a clipped tone. Then he turns to position himself with his butt in my direction.

"C'mon, Vin," I say, "I didn't mean to startle you. C'mon."

"This is harder to tell than the first part of my life," he says, "days are less distinct. My memory is more of times... eras...the Joseph era, the Johnny era, then the living with Johnny era, dating Ray, then living with Ray, then marrying Ray, then having an affair—"

"OK!! OK!!" I say. "I get it. I get it.

"It's hard to have a relationship, Vinny."

"Apparently so. I've never been in a position to prove otherwise."

"Does that make you mad?" I ask him, a little guiltily.

"Oh, I occasionally ponder the notion but I do believe that I am a bachelor at heart . . . You missed a spot," he says, extending his paw to indicate an unoiled portion of the inside ridge of the shoe near the cleat.

"Good eye," I say, dabbing oil on the spot.

Vinny continues his yoga stretching exercises as I search the shoes for other missed spots. After a quiet spell, I stop and turn to Vinny.

"Did you ever . . ." I'm unsure how to continue, wanting to be delicate.

"What?" he asks.

"Well, I just wondered if . . . Well, Sophie is quite an attractive—" A gruff near-growl stops me.

"She is an innocent child . . . My God, that's indecent!" He is disgusted with me. "Really! I can't imagine. Like molesting my sister!"

"Sorry . . . just a question," I stutter.

I try to figure a way to change the subject but before I can, Vinny speaks.

"I can imagine nothing more sensual or erotic than a long, slow belly rub."

His eyes have sealed themselves shut as his head tilts back slowly. I am suddenly uncomfortable, caught in the revelation that Vinny looks at me as a romantic partner. The notion makes me anxious, filling my head with memories of Ray and his jealousy of my cats. I set the snowshoes down and go toward the closet and my duffel bag. I am tripped up by a writhing Sophie on the ground, long, slow undulations that make her slide across the floor like a snake, clearly a work in progress.

"Why does sex make you so tense?" asks Vinny, that bluntly. So bluntly, in fact, that I have no choice but to throw back my head and laugh loudly, as if this illegitimate reaction might somehow legitimately deny his claim.

"Did you know," says Vinny, "that I was nearly crushed on one occasion when you threw Ray off the bed?"

I spin around to face the black cat but am absolutely lost and speechless. I clutch my duffel bag.

"Mere inches," he says, "between my head and his foot..."

Vinny shudders, remembering this old terror.

"So? Do you know why?" he asks after a fair amount of silence. I stare into his blue-green eyes.

"No," I say finally, and put the bag on the table, unzipped, ready for my supplies.

Even Sophie has sensed the change in mood. She has stopped her writhing and settled into a sprawl across the braided rug. She is watching me, waiting. As am I, myself.

IF MY SPEED IS GOOD, it will be at least three days in the snow to the trees and back. The runners on the sled have been sharpened and waxed to make the wood load as light as possible. But even with that, I know I must keep my supplies to a minimum. It will take every bit of strength I have.

I roll the foil space blanket into a tight ball and place it center, easiest access. Around it, I pack my food. Using techniques that Vinny says he learned hundreds of years ago while living as a Scandinavian woodsman, I have cured a portion of our Spam supply. Together, Vinny and I packed it in bread to provide another food source. Then we wrapped the entire thing in brown paper. Vinny has also passed along to me all he learned about trail marking when he lived as an Apache warrior. I will use the brown paper to mark my trail. Lastly, I pack rope, a knife, and the ax. It is all I can think of to bring. I turn to Vinny.

"Sex does not always make me tense, Vinny," I say, but have no idea of what I will say next.

"My mistake," he says in a casual tone, "I thought it did."

"You know, you can be very condescending."

Sophie's head turns back to Vinny, like watching a tennis match, she awaits his return. But he does not return, simply stares at me, the older and wiser.

"It only makes me tense later," I finally utter.

"Later?"

"After a relationship has been going for a while."

"You mean, once you know it could last?"

"Listen, we don't have to talk about this now, do we?" I ask in a commanding sort of way.

"Certainly not," agrees Vinny, "you are much bigger than I am. We can talk about whatever you say."

I stop speaking, shake my head, puzzled at my inability to outwit my cat.

"So," says Vinny as he sprawls across the quilt, "nice weather we're having."

"Oh, knock it off," I say. "We have a lot of work to do before I leave. We have to set up the tent in front of the fireplace."

We have planned a small cave dwelling for Sophie and Vinny. This will conserve the little bit of wood that is left. We have designed it so that Vinny, with thumbless paws, can manipulate wood chips into a small fire that will heat just their camp area and not the whole cabin.

Vinny jumps down off the bed and begins to pace.

"You know, I've been thinking," he says, and then pauses as he continues to walk. He stops and faces me, arching his neck all the way back until his eyes meet mine. "I don't think you should go alone."

Regretfully, I smirk. Vinny's eyes narrow and his stare transforms to a glare.

"What is funny?" he demands.

"It's not funny but I assume you mean you're thinking you should go with me and I just can't imagine you out in that snow," I say, begging forgiveness with every word.

"It's not ideal, I will grant you that, but I have a foreboding sense about this and feel strongly that you should not be alone," he says, and suddenly I sink to a new level of fear about my impending journey.

Vinny turns on a dime and marches himself underneath the bed. I am unsure of what he is doing and think that perhaps he has decided he is too offended to continue but he does not disappear completely. Instead, his butt remains exposed and after a beat he begins to back himself out from under, clearly struggling with something. I watch as he reappears, dragging in his mouth four small woven objects. He gets them to the center of the room and drops them in a pile. I move closer to inspect them as an excited and seemingly proud Sophie begins prancing on her tiptoes.

"What's with her?" I ask as I stoop to pick up one of the objects.

"She helped make them and wants to be sure you know it."

I recognize the woven material as the leather shoelaces from a pair of ancient ski boots that we discovered in the cabin closet. The laces have been shaped into tiny oblongs with a frame made of coat hanger wire. In the center of each object is a patch of leather partially woven into the scheme with a separate piece of shoelace. I don't want to know where the leather came from but am suddenly nervous about the condition of my favorite jacket.

"They should work but obviously I haven't been able to try them on," says Vinny. "Help me on with them, would you?"

I look at Vinny in disbelief.

"Come on, help me on with them. I can't tie a bow to save my life."

I want to protest immediately but cannot imagine how much time this construction must have taken them. I have no choice but to strap him in by the paws.

He has already nosed the four shoes into place and is standing one paw on each leather patch.

"Just wrap the leather so that my paw is completely covered."

Sophie is sitting very nearby, watching every move with eager anticipation. I do as he says.

"Great," he says, "now take that loose lace, wrap it twice around my ankle, and then tie it firmly."

Paw by paw, I secure him into his shoes. When I finish, I stand slowly and step away from him.

"Careful," I say, "it's going to be hard to walk."

Sophie has stood up and sat down several times in her excitement. Vinny takes a deep breath and lifts his front paw. Sophie lets out an encouraging mew. He places forward the first paw and I can tell he has to think hard about which one to lift next, eventually it's the opposite rear. It is not until the third paw has moved that the whole effort fails and Vinny finds himself unexpectedly in a heap on his side.

"Dammit!" he says, obviously somewhat embarrassed. Sophie and I freeze in place.

"Well, somebody help me up!" he orders. I scramble forward and lift him with both hands around his belly. Held in midair, he is able to untangle his legs.

"OK, set me down," he says.

I put him gently on the floor and watch as he repeats his efforts several more times. On the fourth attempt, he has mastered his own coordination but the shoes keep clipping each other, having the effect of Vinny stepping on his own feet, which ultimately trips him up and leaves him in a tangled, fallen mess.

Sophie sighs deeply and lies down. Vinny is hopping mad.

"Dammit! If I make them any smaller they won't hold me above the snow and as they are I can't make my stance wide enough to keep them from stepping on each other. DAMMIT!"

I am afraid to speak. We all stand quiet, Vinny shifting his focus from shoe to shoe, trying to configure a new design.

Finally he speaks softly. "It's no use . . . You're going to have to go on without me." The disappointment in his voice is shattering. Sophie mews.

"It's OK, Vinny," I say. "I'll be OK."

He says nothing but simply stares at the floorboards.

"How about some tea?" I ask.

He shrugs his shoulders ever so slightly but I decide to make it anyway as I know how fond he is of his ginseng. I walk to the kitchen.

"Hey!" he says. I turn to look at him.

"Would you please get me out of these things?"

VINNY IS PRACTICING HIS TECHNIQUE, flipping wood chips into the fire using the catapult system we designed and built with two spoons, a knife, a fork, and some rubber bands. It takes a precise touch and he's having trouble gauging distance. Sophie is alert, aware of the tension that has lingered since the snowshoe incident. She stands by, ready to retrieve his misfires. It is the sum total of all her restraint to return the chips to Vinny's side without falling into a fine game of bat-and-chase.

I can see the frustration in Vinny's brow as he focuses on the task at hand. He judges himself harshly and I know that the snowshoes are weighing heavy on his mind, though his sense of responsibility will not allow him to sulk. He will care for Sophie, keep her safe.

With my back to the cats, I apply pressure to my thigh. I do not want Vinny to know that the throbbing has greatly intensified since this morning. He is worried enough and there is nothing he can do, the time has come for me to go. We cannot afford comfort for each other or ourselves now.

My focus is fixed out the window. I find myself wishing for Vinny's wish, whatever it was. If the dot would only reappear, I could justify not venturing out into the cold.

"What?!" I nearly jump out of my skin when suddenly the black cat with white accents is at my feet, staring at my hand dug into my thigh.

"It's worse, isn't it?" he asks.

"Yes," I say, caught.

Our eyes find each other and I realize that Vinny understands as well as I do that we are pressed against destiny with no choice, no option.

"The last time that I had no choice, my lady, you were at the end of the arm," he says. Then he sits, quietly touching, with the tips of his fur, my leg. We stay like this in stillness as together we travel from soon to now. The time has come, I stand.

"Keep the food outside the heat radius," I say as I pull on the first of the three wool sweaters I have gathered.

"I know," he says.

"Don't let Sophie sit too close to the fire."

"I know," he says.

I pull on sock after sock, then boots, lace them.

"Keep a steady, even pace," says Vinny. "You don't want to push too hard at first. It will wear you down and you'll run the risk of sweating, which will eventually turn to ice."

"I know," I say. I pull on my parka, moving quickly now to ward off the panic that I feel tingling in my fingertips, toes.

"I'll be back in three days at the most," I say as I zip the parka. Vinny nods. Sophie's face looks particularly wide as if she has fluffed herself for my departure. Her eyes round, blinking.

I pull on the backpack and start for the door. Then I turn back.

"Sophie, you be good and do what Vinny tells you."

She blinks again and runs on tiptoes to my feet. She leaps up into my arms and I hold her tight to my chest. She stretches her neck upward and presses her forehead hard against mine and then slowly rubs her cheek against my cheek until her nose touches my ear and I hear her wheezy purr. I pull her back from me, kiss her between her ears, and set her down. She dutifully returns to Vinny and sits behind him.

Vinny and I stare at each other.

"Did we forget anything?" I ask, shrugging my shoulders and trying to smile.

"One would certainly hope not," he answers. He rises from his seated position and walks to my feet. I bend as best as I can with my layers of clothing and struggle to look him in the eye.

"Pick me up," he says. "You're going to strain yourself."

I do as he says. In my arms, I position him so that he can look me in the face.

"Of course you know that you can do this," he says to me.

I nod, waiting for him to tell me more.

"You have a powerful mind and strong spirit, you don't need anything else."

"Except cured Spam," I say, "which, by good fortune, I have."

Vinny shakes his head, unwilling to diminish the moment with glib toss-offs. The forced smile falls from my face.

"Keep me safe, Vinny," I say, with no idea of what I am asking except that I know that my cat understands more of this world than I do and I hope that, somehow, that will help me to survive.

"It's all in your mind," he says, and I know he is telling me to put him down, to go. I hold my face to his, kiss him on the cheek, and set him gently on the floor. I turn and walk to the door, pull my gloves and then mittens over my hands, put my hand on the doorknob, then turn back to my cats. One long blink from each of us and I open the door, fall into whiteness.

BLASTS OF BLINDING ALARM. Everything is gone. There is no before, no after. I am only here. Lean against wind. Bend to driving snow, ice. All my senses filled by cold survival. I turn back, the cabin does not exist. I do not know how long since I left. Was it moments or days?

I press into the wind, pray that I am right about the direction of the sun, buried by so many layers of cloud cast, and I listen to myself, to what I feel. Vinny says I know. It is my instinct that I must trust.

The sled moves quickly and silently. Only that I must keep it regularly cleared of snow do I remember, that it is tied to me, that I am pulling it. So far, I am warm enough. I use the throbbing in my thigh to keep my pace.

Squinting ahead, I see things, then I do not. It is a drift, it is blowing ice, one passes for another in the split second that the eye can open. There dawns a thought that I cannot do this. I squash it. I keep moving.

THE SPACE BLANKET IS FLOATING a hundred feet above me. I stopped to pull it out. Thought I could walk with it wrapped around me. Bones hurt. I can see cold swirling around my individual cells, it's gotten in between the spaces that are in between me. There's cold in places that don't exist. So cold.

At the same second I snapped the blanket open, a huge gust barked and pulled it away from me. It floats above me now on some weird jet stream, idled but whipping madly.

It's difficult to grasp that I might not be able to get warm. I continue walking. To stand still is to die. Always it seems like there's some way to get warmer; turn up the heat, put on more clothes, move more. Here, it might just be too cold.

I stumble occasionally when a stabbing spike of pain shoots through my leg. There's no predicting it. It's a new form of pain. It's running through the center of my bone. The whole thing's gonna blow, feels like.

Still walking. I'm so tired of not being able to see. This constant trusting of my instinct is wearing thin. I want a sign that I am in the right direction. I don't know where I am. I have no idea where I am. Sometimes this thought just passes through and sometimes it gets snagged on some brain tentacle, lingers long enough to blossom into true, blind terror.

Now I'm terrified, happens in an instant. The shudder down my spine is like watching an astronaut tethered against an eternity of floating backward into darkness by one little cable made of some kind of space-age tin. Worse than drowning. Dry drowning.

I've never understood the madness that would allow a person to climb out of a spaceship midcosmos and here I am, blinded and numb. There's nothing to hear but howling wind. I have no senses left, only some kind of inner truth that I've never seen. Stumbling in madness.

NIGHT PASSES FOR DAY HERE. I believe that I have now lived through one night but I have no evidence. I have stopped once for Spam and bread, only long enough to remove it from my sack. Eat in big bites. Remove the wool from my face just long enough to shove it in. If I have survived a night, then I must be near the trees.

Illusions continue to pester me. With no eyes and no ears, it's a mystery where they're coming from. A complete kind of deadness has overtaken my leg but I am calmer than I was. Since the Spam, I have begun to feel some hope that I can make this journey. I don't know where that has come from either. The white and I are learning about each other. I know now how it likes a prank. It acknowledges that I am wise to it.

I am talking to the white when it comes to me that I am standing in brightness. I stop, look down, see lines of definition across the snow. Then I see that I am seeing. This is sun. I look up. This is sun. The snow that surrounds me is only air-borne by wind, nothing falls. I can see it all.

I am laughing, turning in a circle, getting tangled in the sled rope. I face the wind, looking straight on. Trees, the place of color, it is just in the distance. I trust it. The white cannot pull pranks with color, it does not know how. This is sun. These are trees. I was right, with nothing more than faith. I brought myself here on total instinct.

Just beyond an enormous drift, it is all I need to do. Over the drift, to the trees. Get the wood. Turn around. With the sun, with the wood, get to home.

My pace quickened, a near-trot, I head for the drift. I know that it is all farther than it looks, prankster white, but I cannot help myself. Vinny's warning ringing in my head; steady, even pace. I work restraint into my legs, notice a reprieve from the pain in my thigh. Breath, step, step, breath, step, step, head up, breath, step, step, breath—BANG! BAM!!

A clap of thunder, monstrous in its volume. It shakes as much of the world as I can see. It stops me in my tracks. The brightness is fading and from the snowdrift emerges an enormous polar bear.

HIS COAT IS PERFECT WHITE, his teeth a ghoulish yellow. His eyes glow Technicolor and he laughs a wicked taunting squeal at me. He comes closer just by staring.

I am in terror, wrapped in it. Then, as suddenly as the bear has emerged, I laugh at the white.

"What is this," I yell, "some kind of hypothermia vision quest?" and I expect the bear to disappear.

"You got a problem with vision quests, you ugly bitch?! Don't fuck with me! I am your own worst nightmare!"

I am surprised at the duration of this illusion but I play along. "Or what?! You're going to eat me alive?" I shout.

"I won't eat you, you stupid little shit," growls the polar bear, "you'll do that yourself."

I hate this bear. He disgusts me. He fills me with a contempt that has the feeling of an age-old companion. I feel as though I have hated this bear for a very long time.

Suddenly he is much closer. I didn't see him move. Now
he's on me with a hold on my arm, my side. He's attacking, I
think, over and over. He's attacking. He throws me twisting
into the air. I fall with a thud. Now he grabs me under my
arms, lifting me and slamming me into the snow, over and
over.

My thigh is pulsing annihilation. The bear locks his jaw
around my abdomen and with a violent shake throws me with
such power that I force a crater in the snow. In this burrow I
find myself sitting, legs straight out, thigh beating bright,
bright red in the snow, like a turn signal or police lights.

I am in trouble. This illusion is not prankster white.

"You don't scare me, you're a hallucination," I stammer.
Dizzy, I look into his face. "You can't hurt me—you are only
in my mind."

"Oh, the mind!! The mind!!" he shouts. "My favorite tool
of destruction!! Guns don't kill people, brains kill people!!"
He roars with laughter. He steps closer to me, the most massive collection of fur and teeth I have ever seen.

"I ain't no domestic shorthair, silly bitch! You conjured up
a doozy this time; a bad-attitude polar bear with anger for spit
and evil for blood. Meow this, girlie-girl!!" he shouts, and then
grabs his furry crotch.

"I am your worst nightmare!!!" He dances in the snow.

"So you said," I spit at him, "you're repeating yourself—"

"Then I guess it's time to show you!!" and with that he
leaps into the air, commanding the ice and snow and wind to
do the same.

My thigh tightens in excruciating pain. Everything is frozen
and ice except my thigh. It burns, on fire, pulsing bigger and
bigger with a fury inside. I fall back into the snow in a torturous scream of anguish as I feel my leg rip apart from the
inside. I roll my head from side to side and for one second I
am able to glance down toward my leg. It has, as I suspected,
ripped wide open, a gaping hole from crotch to knee, along

an inner seam. Inside is a pulsating ivory white mass, swirling grotesquely in anger and confusion. I cannot look at it, it is vile and disgusts me. It smells like rotten flesh and I feel that the sight of it could kill me.

The polar bear floats above me, laughing. I am screaming in pain and fear. I lock eyes with the bear.

"Make it stop!!!" I scream. "Make it stop!! Take that thing out of my thigh!!!"

This makes him laugh louder. "Help you??!! Help you??!! But don't you see, I've come to watch you die!!"

"Who are you?!" I scream.

"I've watched you build your weapon of destruction for so many years . . . and what a good little weapon builder you are! Very impressive, storing away every last piece of ammunition . . . It's remarkable how you've been able to hold on to every little scrap! It's been torturous for me, though, I'll tell you that. Nothing I like better than a full-fledged, kick-ass self-annihilation!! My only consolation has been knowing that the longer I waited, the more you would store away and the more glorious your decline would be. Oh, baby! You'll never survive this! Not with the power in your arsenal! Yes, ma'am! Let the games begin!"

I scream another howl into the wind and a crash of light breaks across my brain.

I am alone to save myself.

I am alone to purge my thigh.

The pain leaps to a new level. I twist into a convulsive pinch, my head thrust back. Then suddenly I am warm as, from my thigh, stories of my life begin to come.

SHARDS OF COLOR RISE UP from the ivory white mass, swirl around the bear; his hair and teeth swept away into color, into a whirling dervish from which pictures of me emerge, in many shapes and sizes. Images of me now floating where the bear had been only seconds before.

Snapshots, soaked in color, emerging with a rip or a tear, searing pain with each expulsion. I lie, face up, in the snow, tears flowing silently from my eyes. I know there is pain, I feel it every bit, but my brain denies me access to reaction. I am paralyzed to watch as the pictures spew from my thigh, float above me, forming themselves into specific split seconds of memory and then the truth behind the image.

Eleven years old, my father and me sitting side by side in the Buick. My eyes are fixed straight ahead, his focus is on me. His hand fills the space between us, opened, gesturing out at the world. It is a picture of a father and his little girl, a tender moment of togetherness. Then the picture breaks out of its frame, comes alive. My father brakes the car to a crawl and says, "You probably don't think you'll ever stick your hand into a pile of baby shit either, but you will ... when you have to."

"What the hell does that mean?!" I shout, demanding an answer nineteen years too late. I clench crystallized snow in my hand, seething at the truth behind the picture and the ultimate inevitability of changing diapers.

Standing in the hallway at Sunday school; it's a Polaroid of me, my mother, the little boy with hippie parents, and the hippie parents themselves. We are gathered in a circle. My face is wide open in laughter. My mother is smiling at the little boy and the hippie dad is reaching toward me with open arms. I relax in the snow as I stare at this snapshot of warmth and acceptance and then the color begins to seep beyond its edges. My mother steps away and leans down to whisper in my ear, "It doesn't matter what a person wears, as long as it's clean."

As the color mutates from one picture to the next, I am tortured by the bear. He reappears momentarily before taking on the impending image. He eggs me on. He points and laughs.

Now the picture is me with Mom and Dad in the kitchen, a long-ago dusk frozen outside the window behind us. A half-full glass of milk is being held out to me by my mother. Her mouth is frozen in the middle of some word. We are held in laughter. But this time I am not tricked. Seeing the picture, I remember its truth, so different from the way it looked. My mother says, "Bottoms up." I laugh, she laughs, my father laughs and then he says, "I guess it's pretty funny when your bottom's as big as hers."

I want to reach in and shake myself, get myself to stop laughing like an idiot, stand up for myself. The image dissolves into white flurry and I am spitting at its remnants, crying like a little girl.

This is all too clear, like catching an unexpected reflection of myself in a storefront window. The reflected image that shocks and confuses, so different from the way I think I look.

A birthday picture, Mom and me standing in the upstairs bathroom. I am one day shy of eleven and Mom holds a brightly wrapped box with a pink bow. As the picture jumps into motion, I hear myself insisting that I will shave my legs. Mom takes the lid off the wrapped box, an electric razor. She says, "Just remember, once you shave they'll never be soft again. They grow back like bristles."

New picture: Heading up the front walk, I am frozen mid-step, my arms loaded down with bags and books. Dad stands in the doorway, his arms out as if he is greeting me, welcoming me home. Then his mouth begins to move. He says, "You might as well start learning how to live with yourself when you have nothing to do because there'll be a time in life when you'll be alone with nothing to do and you better figure out how you're going to handle it."

A panic overwhelms me. I scan the horizon, strain to see past the hideous polar-bear color, searching for anything good and true. Somewhere I must remember a picture that is as it seems, there must be a picture that works.

"Stop the philosophizing!" roars the bear.

"What do you know?!" I scream back. "You can't know my thoughts." I twitch in the drift.

"I own your thoughts, you stupid cunt!" His gut-wrenching howl reaching new heights.

"Then why torture me?!" I moan.

"Roll the videotape!" he commands. I screech in agony and from my thigh comes more, now in full motion, clips and sound bites.

My father, arriving home from work, notices I have lost weight. Mom says, "Look. She's got curves."

"I like that!" screams the bear as he transforms out of me and back into his likeness.

"I don't care what you like!" I glare at him and then spit into his fur. This seems to stun him. He looks at me, and for a split second he is little and confused. Then he isn't.

"Silly, silly, girlie-girl. You just don't get it, do you?" and he sends himself spinning backward, pulling color shards from my thigh into his center with a maniacal centrifugal force.

I am fourteen. I have a tick; an elongated blink that keeps my eyes closed for seconds at a time. My father says, "The world won't disappear, you know."

Then I am in the family room, watching fourteen-year-old Nadia Comaneci sail through the air.

I say, "Everyone says she's so young. I'm fourteen, nobody says I'm so young."

"You're not competing on a world stage," says Mom.

They come faster now, one on top of the next. I brace myself, fight for control over my memory. All around me, snow is melting. The heat of simmering bile; racing raging anger at the misinterpretation, misinformation, misunderstanding.

I'm a fat nine-year-old. I have one pair of pants that fit well. They make me feel almost normal. I wear them all the time. My father appears and says, "You've got your uniform on, I see."

I am verging on blackness, complete shutdown, the pain so complete.

Seventh grade, days into a bout of depression brought on

by a movie called *The Other Side of the Mountain* about the paralyzed Olympic skier Jill Kinmont. My teacher says, "You have to learn to separate yourself from the things you see."

Tears of confusion roll down my face.

"This is all wrong!" I scream at the bear. "You're slanting the evidence! I don't hold my childhood in contempt! These are passing comments of no importance! It has all been misconstrued!!"

The bear reappears. He is rock still. He stares at me, an expectant glint in his eye.

"It's your memory," he finally says, and for a split second he seems unsure of how to proceed. In his hesitation I see something new before me.

It is my memory. He is right. I am stunned at the thought. These are the pictures that I framed so tightly that I kept the truth living behind them safely tucked away. This is linguistic input, throwaway language that has lodged in my brain. Words unimportant, moments incidental, forgotten by their speaker, remembered only by me as they adhered to my psyche and changed my perception.

These are the echoes in my brain. It's what I can't forget but don't remember. Definitions and negations equaling, in the end, an empty set, null and void.

"STOP, BEAR," I SAY QUIETLY. The bear stands frozen and quiet. His response secures what I suspect. Like everything else, the picture of the bear and the bear are two very different things. Only I know the things he has shown me, only I know the fact and fiction of it all. If he were truly a separate entity, he would have no idea.

"I know who you are," I growl, "and I won't take this crap anymore."

We are at a standoff. It's me against my rage. My bear's eyes dart quickly left to right, logging getaways.

"Too late for that, bear boy! You're in this for keeps now. I got you and you got nowhere to go!"

The polar bear rears up on his hind legs, beats his chest with his front paws. He lets out a roar that shoots across the sky, turns white cirrus to black nimbus.

"I'm not afraid!!" I roar back as I struggle to pull my head and shoulders up and out of the snow.

I know I must rein my bear in, take charge of my own demise. I stiffen my arm and stretch it down along my body. I take a deep and frightened breath, and then plunge my hand into the writhing wound of my own thigh. Gasping in pain, I push deeper and deeper until my hand is submerged in the mass. One tough yank and my fist emerges holding, like a snowball, a pulsating, fiery ball of incensed confusion. Eyes locked on whiteness, I hurl the ball into the face of the bear.

"You are only the tip of my iceberg, bear boy! You don't know the half of my fury!!"

Covered in my fuming rage, the bear stares at me in disbelief. Then, without warning, he crumples into a shaking pile of pelt and tears.

"What'd you have to do that for?" he wails.

"Fix my leg!!"

"I can't do that! I'm just the messenger." He continues to bawl.

"Oh, stop crying, you insipid little bear. Get over here and help me!"

He hobbles close, unsure in his new role.

"What do you want from me? I don't know how to fix this. You made it!"

"This is no time to point fingers. Take it out of my leg!!"

The bear pulls back, his head shaking, a look of frightened disgust on his face.

"Oh, come on, you coward! Pull it out for me!!"

"I don't know how . . . You have to do it . . ."

"What are you talking about?! You were doing fine just a few minutes ago!"

"That was all an act. I was just egging you on. You've been doing it all along. I just scared you into starting...That's all I know how to do..." He has diminished into a little bit of nothing.

"Besides," he whimpers, "you didn't have to throw it at me...did ya?"

"Jesus! What a worthless tower of strength you turn out to be. Just sit there and shut up."

I shift my disappointed gaze away from him and stare at the mess of my leg. It is my job now to empty this thigh of its poison. Beyond anger, now, beyond fear, this is a showdown, full disclosure. I am cold and weak and know that my time is not endless. Face-off.

One by one, with my own hand, deep into my wound. I pluck out the guarded, the shunned, the frightened and ashamed. Pictures buried to last a lifetime. Ancient eyes squint at the light.

In my hand, a small girl in pink peg-legged denims. She is scrambling to pull up her pants, tuck in her striped stretchy shirt. She yells after the sound of laughing boys; a brother and friends.

"You said you wouldn't tell!! You promised!!" She is running after them now.

She crouches behind a station wagon, crawling on hands and knees to stay out of view. She listens as the boys tell her mother how she pulled down her pants and gave them all a look.

I can feel her indignation like a brand-new feeling. She's been tricked. She had understood them to all be on the same side. They wanted to see it. She wanted to show it. A common bond. They were wonderful, fun boys as they ran together toward the enclave in the bushes. She was proud when she took down her denims and squatted to show them what she possessed and then she looked up into three frightened faces, furrowed her eyebrows, and laughed. She stood, ready for their next adventure. But before she could even hike up her britches, they were gone. Running toward home, Mom, and a cowardly betrayal. She was left alone to calm herself, configure a response, recapture her dignity.

The bear sobs quietly and reaches out a paw, tries to comfort the little girl, console her. But she floats just out of reach, where she lingers amid flurries, ready to watch as the rest of the story unfolds.

I DIG BACK INTO MY THIGH. Now that little girl has grown a few inches, quickened the flick of her eye. She steps from my leg, yelling. In a plaid dress, she holds a pair of blue trousers in her hand. In an instant, I know the story she is here to tell.

It is 1969. She is seven. Second grade. She screams about her year-end field trip to Blanford Nature Center; trail hikes through the woods with birds and bugs and a picnic outside on blankets spread across a field.

She begs her mother to allow her to wear pants on that day. She screams and cries, fights with all of her might. I lift my hands up out of the snowdrift, try to push her forward, support her fight. But finally she is told that this is still a school day and she will wear a dress with knee socks and brown orthopedic school shoes and certainly, she is assured, all the other good girls will do the same.

And they do. I watch as they appear in full dress; plaids and stripes, rickrack and pleats, and, of course, that colored string that runs across undeveloped tits, scrunching up the material into a hundred little ridges that take forever to break in.

They spend the last school day of second grade leaping and howling through fields of flowers, looking like a band of trailblazing debutantes.

Then my little girl stands in a new classroom, the first day of third grade. She wears boys' tennis shoes with her dress. Then the setting dissolves into my fourth-grade classroom, and without my girl moving a muscle, she is wearing pants.

I gasp out loud as I see a painful confusion seep into my little girl's eyes. I know she is remembering her lost battle in second grade. Everywhere she looks there are little girls wearing pants, only pants.

Little girls wear little boys' clothes now and nobody has said the first thing about it. She hasn't been given a single explanation. She simply doesn't wear rickrack and pleats anymore. I watch her store away this tiny confusion to a place where it will grow. She walks a new walk toward her new desk, pants being freer than skirts. I watch her hesitate as she finds a new way to sit, feet wrapped around the legs of her chair, no more sense of opened legs.

"A brand-new dance and nobody knew how to teach it," I say out loud.

"Pardon," says the bear.

"What?"

"You said something," he tells me.

"Did I?"

My awareness is shifting. I think that I may be dying but I'm so cozy, tucked in my snowdrift, so relaxed, that I have trouble sticking to that thought, seeing it through. Instead, I let a calm breath escape my lips as my mouth arcs upward toward pleasure. I float. Anesthetized ecstasy.

THE STORIES CONTINUE; me always, from barely born to grown, smocking to stockings. A wave of release undulates down my spine and I watch my third grader bounce a red rubber ball hard on the asphalt-covered road of the playground.

It is a morning recess in the spring of 1970. As I lie in the snow, I am overcome with the fury of that morning—the first time I felt that rage.

It's Four-Square season. A game played with a ball in a square grid made up of four smaller squares numbered 1, 2, 3, 4. The ball is allowed only one bounce in a square before it must be hit into another square. When a player misses, that player must leave the game and a new player enters at the first square. The goal of the game is to reach and maintain the fourth square.

I look around the playground, it's alive with puffed-up little boys who know they can pick their game and make the fourth square in the first round of any of them. I watch as, game after game, girls succumb to unfair advantages allowed the boys.

I grab the bear by the neck hairs, scream at him as I watch the scene unfold, "Boys wore jeans! Girls wore dresses!"

"It's not my fault," cries the bear.

"We were just starting to wear Jack Purcell tennis shoes instead of brown orthopedic lace-ups!! Just starting!! We weren't used to the maneuverability—there was no way!!" I am tightening my grip on his throat.

"I believe you!! Let go!!!" He is shivering in fear.

"But beyond the Purcells, we had to keep in mind bare knees and visible underwear. The boys could lunge—we could skip—the boys could spin—we could twist—how could you expect to see a dress in the fourth square??!! How?!"

"You couldn't!! Absolutely not!" And with that he wrangles free.

I watch my third grader as she waits for her chance. I know she will make it to the fourth square, I remember the feeling so completely—the fourth square, the highest square, the square of supreme control. She is fighting for my life against three boys convinced the momentary victory is a fluke.

It's ferocious. Every other hit is into her square—slap, spin, spike, skid—they try every tactic they know but her playing is inspired.

Out goes Ned Smith, square 1, in comes Jeff Chambers, square 1. Out goes Bill Ray, square 2, in comes Scott Spence, square 1. Out goes Bob Strong, square 3, in comes Dale Dixon. She is reigning proudly as she flattens Jeff Chambers and sends him running to the boys' barrel in search of his ego. Scott Spence moves to the third square, Dale Dixon to the second, and the first square opens up for the next competitor.

I feel the muscles in my body contract against the snowdrift as I watch Donna Perkins step into the first square. I watch my third grader's face and I know what she is thinking—this is it—this is our moment—we will finally rule...

She turns to Donna for a silent moment and that's when it happens—Donna starts to whine—whine and giggle—and fidget and whimper—about the ball being thrown too hard—and running and throwing and getting hit...

I am mesmerized as I watch my girl stand in the fourth square in utter disbelief, the ball held between hip and forearm, fuming. The fury is building rapidly now—I see it in her—I feel it in me. In a burst of movement—I wheel the ball out from under my arm, lift it high in the air, and spike it hard against the asphalt. It sails up into the air and stays there. I roar, "JUST PLAY THE STUPID GAME!"

Donna's entire body lifts up off the ground and moves backward. There is no visible effort. She just blows away.

The bear is rocking himself forward and back, coiled into a big bear ball. He looks autistic and I tell him so.

"Cut it out!" I say. "It's disturbing."

"All this yelling," he moans, "everyone who comes out of your leg is yelling. I find it very upsetting. All this conflict..." He fades into a whimper.

"Well, I'm sorry for that, ol' bear, but there just wasn't time for Donna's weakness...," I tell him. "Nobody is screaming without just cause."

"Let's just sit quiet for a moment, can we?" So pathetic in his plea that I have no choice but to grant his wish. I fly in the breeze, I am adrift, incapable of true discord.

So we are quiet. Snow falls.

IT IS NOT BECAUSE I intend it that another little me sneaks from my thigh and creeps to the crevice of my knee. That is just her way, forever peeking at the forbidden; a mother and father in a dark room making bedsheets rustle, a horseback-riding teacher and her boyfriend in the high school parking lot during a football game, big kids in the back of the bus folded in on each other in early morning darkness. She is the peeker.

The bear and I watch as she gathers information, trying to solve the discrepancy between the desires she sees in others and the ones she feels in herself. She is by nature an observer, from the outside, thinking she will never want to do these things. Not the natural way of things for her. It is curious, interesting, and foreign. The big kids in the back of the bus, there is nothing in their kiss that rings familiar.

She watches with obsessive fascination, one species observing another; look at the raccoon wash its food, see the ape groom its baby, watch the boy kiss the girl, watch the girl like it. In her face, fear and desire, repulsion and excitement, confusion and clairvoyance.

Suddenly she stands, fully revealed, and announces, "I won a kissing contest in school today between Valerie and me. Jeff said I was a better kisser during a science movie in the auditorium that all the second graders had to watch."

My mother appears, silent, hands on hips, lips pursed.

"Pretty good, huh?" she says.

"I don't think so," says my mother.

The life in my little girl's face disappears, she slips back down behind my knee.

She is watching when I emerge in my favorite pair of pants, carrying a fourth grader's schoolbooks. I sit on a bench and a dark-haired girl with horn-rimmed glasses appears next to me. Delilia Rockland tells me that babies come from a woman when a boy pees inside her.

"How do you know?" I demand, horrified.

"It's true," she says, "when you have a baby, you're going to have to let a boy pee in you. My mom says it's nice if you know you're going to get a baby."

"No boy is ever going to pee in me!" I announce.

I am in bed, my mother tucking me in.

I say, "How could you let that happen to you?"

Then there are the words: *vagina, penis, sperm, eggs.* My mother tells me, night after night, that it's a long way off and it's only right when you're in love, married, and only, ever, with one man. She tells me there are ways to keep babies from coming and some boys force themselves on girls and there are ways to keep babies from coming and it's always best to wait. She says only when you're sure, only when there's love, only with your husband, only when you're old.

I sit in the mall, watch men and women walk together. I stare them down; they've done it, they do it all the time, they did it last night.

I am in my bed, I tell my mother, "I don't want to do it."

She is pleased.

Then I tell her I have figured out another way to keep babies from coming. I will glue lots of pins to the end of a cork. I will put it up inside me. My mother says that isn't quite the point. I tell her I am certain that it will keep boys and babies away. Then I tell her about all the people at the mall and how many of them I believe have done it.

Her face is worried when she says that we have talked enough about this. I am lying in my bed wondering what went wrong with my cork.

"Hey!!" yelps the bear. "Girl!!"

His sound shatters my vision. A swift gust of wind sweeps the color away. I am left in white.

"You don't look so good, and I'm hungry... I think we have to figure something out," says the bear in a kind of "duh, I dunno" tone.

I am freezing cold, wet, and near dead. My mouth opens stiffly but I cannot hear my scream, lift my head, move my arms. Buried alive, snow zombie. My eyes, the one thing I can move, summon the bear close. He creeps toward me on little bear toes, leans in with an awkward delicacy. His breath is so wicked that it shocks my consciousness. Softly I whisper, "We have to get the wood."

"Oooohhhhh, no, no, nooooo...," he wails, falling back on his haunches, "we're gonna die!"

I shoot commando rays into his soul with my eyes and he goes silent, leans in again.

"What?" he asks again, same intensity, sound coming through his big stopped-up nose.

"Put me on the sled," I demand, "and take us to the trees now!"

He is whimpering, hanging his head, dragging his paws, but doing as I demand. When he lifts me, I am surprised and warmed at his gentleness. I take this opportunity to whisper in his ear.

"You gotta stay mad," I mumble, and feel the effect immediately. He runs on my blind anger, this bear. I must keep him fueled with fury, I think.

I am loaded onto the sled and watch as he takes his place at the helm, the sled rope held in his massive jaws. As he makes a first step, I feel the runners break away from the cold snow and slip into a glide. We are moving. I fade away.

A jerk wakes me. Through squinted eyes, I see the bear pulling the sled. I see that we have just peaked the ridge of the drift and are headed down the other side. I see trees are green. We are running now, flying across snow, sky is racing, green is growing, closing in. White.

Open my eyes under green leaves. We are not moving. I roll my head and watch as fuzzy lines come to solid, slur into pastel. Hold still. The bear comes into view. He is standing, staring at the tree, leaning a paw against the bark, tapping bear fingers. He turns back to check on me. The confusion in his face, epic. He is lost.

I remember what I have learned. He is fueled by rage and I am the pipeline. I conjure up an image. I color brain waves in bright reds and yellows, send them up into the sky to dance. It is a picture of me running toward the tree, climbing it. Behind me I draw the school-yard boys who chased the girls at recess. They chased the girls to capture them, drag them to the boys' barrel, and hold them hostage, to force them to kiss the boys.

The bear rips off tree limbs as he climbs, throws them to the ground. The bully boys howl, push, and grab like wild animals as they run. My bear forges ahead, full tilt now. He is watching tree branches when the truth behind the image appears. He is not looking when the boys pass me by in hot pursuit of other girls. He does not understand where the anger really lives, it sits between two points that cannot be reconciled; the just indignation of being chased and the bitter loneliness of not being chased.

Higher and higher my bear goes, never looking back, still running from the bullies I have conjured. The branches are thinner and weaker with every step. Onto my sled the wood comes raining down, stacking in piles around me, making a little sled cabin.

Then comes a sharp crack! I see the bear in free fall above me. He is gaining speed despite the tree limbs that break his flight. His big bear arms and legs flailing, he cannot get ahold. Instantly, I draw one of the bully boys beneath him, standing on the strongest branch I can see. I make the bully scream and jeer, louder and louder. The bear throws an angry arm in the bully's direction, a final desperate attempt to hurt my tormentor, and with three clawed fingers, my bear finds a grasp. The fury of his fear, using teeth and claws to cling, dissolves the bully into dust. He uses every last bit of him to gain ahold. Like stardust, the bully ash falls upon me and I am blanketed from the cold, safe from exposure.

"Good work, bear boy."

He grins big. "Are you warm?" he asks.

I look down at my bully-ash blanket and then back up at him. I nod.

"We need to get back to the cabin," I whisper, "and you need to check that the wood is secure before we move."

The bear gives a slow nod of the head and then continues to stare at me.

I stare back, realizing I must give him his power. I close my eyes, working hard to stay conscious, while I make the picture that will make him mad.

Above me, against a cold blue sky, a vision of me appears. I sit on a bar stool. I am shifting, trying coolly to pull down the leather miniskirt that is riding uncomfortably high on my thigh. I am trying my best to be "that kind of girl" but am so inexperienced that I can actually feel the makeup as it sits on my face.

Next to me, another bar stool appears and next to that stands a guy named Al.

Al is talking to someone on his other side but I hardly hear him. Al sells things, stocks maybe, water purifiers maybe, I don't know.

I am sitting at the bar, three cocktails in, when he sits down on the stool beside me and turns his head in my direction. Like a slow-moving train, he starts in on these stocks ... or the water purifiers. I don't know because when I turn to look at him, a windblown Ken doll from deep in New Jersey, I realize in a startling flash of clarity that I am devoid of sex. I have no definition. I have been raised but not grown. There is nowhere but a strip mall to tell me who I am. No one but a Barbie doll to tell me how to stand. Nothing but a leather skirt to tell me how to feel.

I stare at him, hear nothing, watch his lips move—thinking I have no reference point for this. Knowing I don't know how to be picked up and knowing I don't want to learn from a guy named Al and knowing how desperately I want to know. Anything that might help to start a line, some definition, something more than "female."

I look like an idiot. I gaze up into his face in a deaf stupor. Then he stops talking, my hearing clicks on, and he says, "You remind me of that girl Cissy from *Family Affair*."

My gaze drops, the vodka in my belly flip-flops as a wave of disgust at being compared to the most sexless, edgeless girl who has ever existed moves through me. My head starts to pound as a second revelation sinks in, this caveman thinks it's a compliment. I take a deep breath, let it out slowly, and say, "No, I don't. You're just saying that."

I want to vomit. In his eyes, I see myself flailing. I take a final swig of my cocktail. I have every intention of leaving. I stand up, grab my bag, and Al says, "You're so clean I could eat off you."

My head snaps back as the sled starts to move. I can hear a growl growing within the belly of my bear.

Above me, against the cold blue sky, the bar stools vanish and I am floating in the air. On my back, a leather miniskirt bunched up around my waist, Al's face between my legs, smashed up into me, gnawing, making noises like a dead engine trying to turn over. My eyes are wide open, I stare up toward space, thinking about stocks and water filters.

The rope pulls tight. My bear breaks into a full run. Clouds slip by faster and faster. His tanks are full with the fury of hopelessness, the anger of ambivalence.

I feel a softness settling upon me as I let go of some very old shame. I'm perched on the tip of an expensive high, the perfect state of falling, after the fear and before the ground. This is the grace in surrender. The moment is sweet, so sweet that I think I cannot open my lungs enough to take in the enormous breath that I feel.

It's a chilly stillness that wakes me. Peeking out from under my lids, I watch as the bear rolls lazily in a snowbank. We are at a dead standstill. I have no sense of how long we've been here. I call up my strength.

"Hey!" I choke out a hoarse whisper. The bear stops midroll, turns his great big head in my direction.

"What are you doing?" I ask. "Why are we stopped?"

The bear sits up and furrows his brow. I can tell he's taking a stab at thinking. The vacant look on his face when he finally brings his eyes back around to mine tells me that he has failed. His shoulders climb into a shrug and then I remember the sweetness of letting go. Al and his water purifiers had gotten us this far. Releasing my humiliation and the resulting ecstasy has stopped us in our tracks.

The thought of more anger makes me tired. I feel empty and unable to conjure up more rage. Then, suddenly, almost as if he had created an idea all on his own, the bear speaks.

"Do you have any food? Bear cannot live on rage alone," he states.

I nod and gesture toward the bag that is strapped down at my feet.

"There's Spam and bread in my bag," I tell him. With more focus and enthusiasm than I have seen since the moment we met, he dives for the bag.

"Very, very hungry!" he exclaims. As he pulls at the ropes that hold down the bag, he turns to looks at me.

"What's Spam?" he questions.

"Don't ask."

He is rough with the bag and I am afraid he will rip it apart in his excitement.

"It's right on top, open it gently," I tell him.

Like a child, he hunkers down and claw by claw tries his best to be delicate. With one extended claw, he skewers the Spamcakes, sets the bag down as lightly as he can, and tiptoes his extended paw, with Spam, over to me.

"Good job," I say when he finally makes it through to the food. He takes half the contents of the package and pops it into his mouth all at once.

"Where's the rest?" he asks me as he licks his chops, his paw about to toss back the last half in a second bite.

"That's all there is. I hadn't expected to feed a bear."

His arm freezes in midair, holding the last hunk of Spam and bread aloft like an offering to the gods. He lowers it and looks at it, then looks at me, then back at the Spam, then to the snow. He slowly brings his gaze back to me.

"Do you want some too?" he asks.

Everything in me is wanting to tell him no, let him enjoy what little there is. But the survivalist in me, the animal, knows that I am walking a dangerous edge at this very second and that I need the food.

"Just let me have one bite," I finally say, "and then you can finish the rest."

Without prompting, he inches his way over to me. With two claws, he rips off a human bite-size hunk and carefully places it in my half-open mouth. I chew slowly, having to think through every move. As I swallow, I look at the bear. He is lying back against the snowbank, scratching himself, his food long gone.

"Spam is excellent," he says. "You have to tell me what a Spam looks like. I would like to kill one and have some more."

I close my eyes and say, "Later. We have to go now."

FORWARD WE GO. Again with the wind and the speed and the cold. I am fueling bear boy with snippets. It's all I can muster. I tried using sins against humanity as a whole: Bosnia, the Holocaust, Chernobyl. He was unresponsive, doing little more than taking his position, maybe picking up the rope. These atrocities get us nowhere. I make better time with incidents closer to home.

I am slightly disappointed with my bear and his piddly response to the monumentally horrific disasters that I have conjured, nightmares that have changed the course of history. They do not move him and I fear that he is shallow. However, I am also slightly touched at his loyalty. His righteous anger on my behalf.

From underneath my bully-ash blanket a dark black cloud rises up, hangs above me. It floats high into the sky and as it slips out of sight, sparkle dust blows across the clouds. I feel a release in my thigh. Focusing down, I watch as the enormous mound under my blanket—my hugely swollen, still-open thigh—seems to shrink ever so slightly, the pain decreasing by tiny bits.

In that same instant I wonder just how many thousands of tiny upsets, harsh words, and silent slaps are embedded in my muscles, blended with my blood. I could send my bear around the world with anger at the incidental.

I have clicked on the municipal file in my brain. I'm surprised at the depth of storage space and logged items. It's chock-full of fuel for the bear: parking tickets, fare hikes, jury duty, tax penalties, tow trucks. We keep a steady gait as I simply release one injustice after another.

We have just passed under the space blanket, still afloat on its weird jet stream. I am pleased at having left a marker, a confirmation of my journey. It seems so much quicker, the journey home. It always does.

Even though my thigh hangs open—gaping, masses of muscle, nerve missing—the pain is tolerable because I know what it is now. Now it feels like truth.

The sky sails by above me. The white is my friend. There's a music in the wind. Something inside me is beginning to ascend. The view is improving.

GREEN. THE WHITE IS GONE. The white is green. I search the periphery for a sliver of white. My stomach rolls, my fingers burn, I sweat. This is panic. The white is gone. I am unprotected. My breath jams in my throat. On my skin, air sits gently. Then I recognize the sensation, I am warm.

My head rolls, side to side. I force my eyes open and there at my shoulder sits Vinny. His gaze intense, a damp cloth hangs heavy from his mouth. He sees my eyes open and his head begins to beat a slow nod. I lift up, look toward the window, and there the green comes again.

Then I remember the sled, slowing to a stop. The bear lifting me up, cradling me in his arms, his repeated chant, "We're home. We're home." And on the horizon, green rolling in. The dot no longer missing, it is nearly arrived.

"The dot, bear, the dot!" I said to him.

"You shouldn't talk," he told me, "I think you're almost dead."

"Almost here, the dot . . . ," I said, "almost . . ."

I lie back against the pillow, look hazily at Vinny. He lets the cloth drop gently across my forehead. My eyes close. Vinny says, "Sssshhhh."

A deep black darkness seeps across the edges of my inner vision, obliterating the sight that comes with shut eyes. In the center of my vision I see the word uttered by my bear: "home." It flashes on, then off, then on; "home...home... home."

"Where am I?" I ask, and then I am certain that I have not been home for a very, very long time.

I EMERGE FROM THE TOTAL BLACKNESS to a slow rhythm of a crackling fire. The hiss pulls me up out of my deep sleep and my eyes open easily. Then I recognize the deeper rhythm of Sophie's wheezy purr. She is curled at my neck, her nose to my ear, as if she is trying to breathe a life back into me. She sees my eyes open and begins a feverish series of head bangs against my cheek, neck, mouth.

"Settle down, Sophie," I hear Vinny say, "you'll suffocate her."

Sophie obeys. She nuzzles into the nape of my neck and stays there, slowly stretches a paw out across my chest so that she holds me in a tiny little hug.

I turn in the direction of Vinny's voice and find him sprawled in front of the fire with the bear stretched opposite him. Evidence of an ongoing card game sits between them.

"Go fish," Vinny says.

The bear cocks his head, says, "What?"

"That's how you play the game! I'm not going to say it your way anymore," Vinny says, irritated.

"What?" grunts the bear.

"Go SALMON fish!" Vinny finally snorts. "You are so annoying!"

The bear smiles broadly, rocking himself from side to side. Then with his index claw, he skewers a card from the middle pile.

A boisterous meow comes out of Sophie, Vinny's head

snaps around. He sees me and quickly leaves his cards, which lie facedown in front of him, jumps onto the bed.

"Can you hear me?" he shouts.

"Of course I can hear you," I say to him. He seems surprised.

"Who am I?" he asks hesitantly.

"Vinny? What's the matter with you?"

His eyes pop wide open. "You're really awake!"

"Of course I'm awake."

"Easy for you to say. I've been watching over you for five days," he says. "I have to tell you, I thought you were crossing over into another dimension."

"I've been back for five days?!" I don't remember anything.

Suddenly I am aware of some impending responsibility, some job I've missed. Without missing a beat, Vinny says, "Our guest has not arrived yet. The dot stood still for several days. It only started moving toward us again this morning."

I let out a sigh of relief. There is a connection somewhere in my brain between the dot and home, to the key that will let me in.

"Don't worry," says Vinny, "you haven't missed a thing."

Sophie has lifted her head and stares into my face. Her purr is a roar. Little splatters of kitty spit fall on my cheek.

"She's glad you're back," says Vinny. Sophie slides her nose along my lip and rests her forehead on my face.

"Hungry?" Vinny asks.

Suddenly I realize I'm famished.

"Go fish!" cries the bear, unaware that anything else has transpired outside his card game.

"Oh shut up, Simon," says Vinny.

"Simon?" I ask.

"Yes?" answers the bear, so dopey he's not even confused.

"Your name is Simon?" I ask.

Now he looks perplexed, uncertain of what he thought he knew.

"Yes, his name is Simon," says Vinny in a tired tone.

"I didn't know he had a name. So I guess I don't have to introduce you."

"Oh, I've known Simon forever," says Vinny.

"You mean before now?"

"Forever," repeats Vinny.

I glance at Vinny, unsure of what he is telling me.

"He's always been around, you just never noticed him," Vinny says in a casual tone. "Dumb as a stump but, all things considered, not a bad bear."

"He saved my life," I say.

"Well, then, that's a good thing. Now what about some food for you?"

"Anything," I tell him.

"I'm afraid the only thing I can get for you is Spam," Vinny says. "Everything else requires thumbs."

"Spam!" shouts Simon. "You have Spam here?! You did not tell me you had Spam, Vinny! I love Spam!"

"He ate my Spam," I tell Vinny, and fuzzy pictures of the journey begin to float in my head. "He's quite fond of it."

Vinny shakes his head, rolls his eyes, and sets off to prepare me a lunch. Simon crawls up onto the bed and lies next to me.

"It's good that you are not dead," he tells me.

"Yeah," I say, "I think so too."

Sophie has stiffened a little with Simon's approach.

"It's OK, Soph," I tell her, "he won't hurt you."

"I like cats," says Simon, and he pats Sophie on the very top of her head, bouncing her a little with each tap.

She slithers away and shoots down to the other end of the bed, under the blankets. There her soft fur touches my foot and I can feel the steady vibration of her purr. She is safe and secure, I think.

I look across the cabin, at its floorboards, at its walls and corners, hoping these details will lift me from the melancholy I feel settling in around me. I am slipping softly down into it as I try to count backward to the last time I felt safe, secure. I wonder if Sophie considers herself at home right now, right here.

"Thank you for getting me back, Simon," I say after a silence.

"It was my job," he responds.

"Yes," I say, and we lie together in quiet warmth.

THIS TIME IT IS A ROUGH PULLING at my thigh that awakens me. I jerk my leg away and hear a startled meow. Looking down, I see Vinny and Sophie licking the wound on my leg.

"It must be kept clean," says Vinny, and he turns to Sophie. "Keep licking."

"Can't we use a washcloth?" I ask.

"Not as effective," he replies.

"It hurts."

"Of course it hurts. OK, that's enough for now."

Sophie jumps down off the bed and makes a leap onto the windowsill.

"The dot?" I ask.

"I suspect it's about a day away," Vinny tells me.

"I'm cold."

"Simon!" Vinny commands, "More wood!"

Simon leaps to attention. "More wood!" and he galumphs out the door.

"How do you know him again?" I ask.

"Oh my, let's see ... He's been around since before I was wandering the deserts and that was several hundred years B.C.—but I've been in touch with him this time around too. I'm sorry I never introduced you." Vinny is pondering his answer.

"How come everyone's got past lives but me?" I demand.

"You do," he replies.

"I don't remember anything."

"There is only so much that can come from knowing one's past lives," says Vinny in an attempt to comfort me, "aside from handy fishing tips or, say, how to make sun tea . . . The real advantage is knowing where your knowing stops. You, for example, had to start from scratch this time around."

"And you?" I ask him, wanting to nail down a full understanding of his wisdom.

"Oh, heavens," he says, "I knew from the git-go that I would be facing some major control issues. I've been quite powerful in many of my previous incarnations and I'm not sure I've always handled myself in an honorable way."

"Napoléon," I say.

"Exactly. I'm glad you understand."

"So, it's just one long journey until you get it right?" I confirm.

"Them's the rules as I understand 'em," Vinny says with a sigh, "exhausting stuff."

"And are you almost there?" I ask him.

"I hardly think so. There are hundreds of creatures far simpler than a cat."

"You have to be every single creature before you reach the end?" I'm amazed.

"Oh, no," he says, "and I have to qualify what I'm saying. Obviously, it is based only on what I have seen and experienced."

"That's OK," I tell him.

"There's a ladder of sorts that every soul climbs but each soul uses different rungs. For example, a zebra and a horse could very well be at approximately the same point in their journey but if they live well, chances are good that they will not return as the other. Ideally, the zebra will not return as a horse, and if he does," Vinny smirks, "he's likely to be quite a cranky horse."

"Like having to do third grade over?" I ask him.

"I suppose. That's why I was more than a little surprised when I found myself as a kitten. I have always considered cats to be a superior species, wildly independent, kings if you will."

"I will," I say. "I've always thought cats had the finest physical design too; graceful, strong, fast, cute."

Then, as if to confirm my belief, Sophie makes a great leap into the air, twisting as she lands, falling into a full body roll, then races for cover under the bed.

"She really does have quite a good sense of humor," says Vinny.

"Anyway, returning as a cat—I honestly didn't consider myself that far along and certainly didn't think it would help me evolve with regard to my particular issues. So, as you can well imagine, I was slightly concerned several days into this life when my eyes opened and I looked at my mother and saw that she was a cat. I thought perhaps I had misunderstood my entire journey. And to make matters worse, I was such a sure little kitten, born to lead, as Mom liked to say. But my original suspicions were confirmed when Little Orange disappeared. I had no control. You see, a cat in a city was a far cry from the cat in my mind."

He is quiet for a little while.

"A far different picture," he says finally.

"Go on," I say, wary, understanding more than ever the deep danger of pictures.

"Well, I believe I've told you this part already. Since that moment, I have had no will of my own, no sense of control. I have had only the choice of acceptance and that's a very quiet thing."

Time passes as we sit. I am awash in revelation. Images of my journey into the snow cloud my eyes. I hear the yelling that so upset Simon, the discord of so many mes all screaming against each other, nothing *accepting* about any of them. It occurs to me then that a quiet thing, such as Vinny mentioned, can only happen from within the body. It's the only way to ensure the silence, to be still from inside and wait for resolution. My concentration begins to break as I try to conjure up a seat comfortable enough for such a long and lonely sit. Then I see that it is not the seat that must be so comfortable in stillness, it is the sitter. Simon begins to growl.

Suddenly Vinny looks at me.

"And thumbs! Of course, no thumbs! Something both you and I overlooked in our admiration of the cat. Thumbs are power," he says.

He shakes his head slowly. "The King of Leverage wears a Crown of Thumbs!"

I nod, having no choice but to remain silent. Finally, I muster up my response.

"So humans are at the top of the ladder, I guess. Is that why souls come back so many times as humans? Because at that point, it's a matter of enlightenment nuances?"

Vinny's look is filled with compassion. "I'm afraid it's the other way around. Just starting out. Which is why it takes so long to get the hang of it."

"What?!" I don't know if I'm angry or relieved. "Then what's on the top?"

"Amoebas, protozoans; those folks." Vinny nods. "Simplicity is the key here."

"Amoebas?! They've got no brains!"

"Exactly. Pure instinct. Not a thought in their cell."

"So what are you saying? The dumber the better? Simon is evolved?" I am feeling suddenly agitated, duped.

"No. Simon is just plain stupid. He's got quite a long road ahead of him," Vinny says. "Bears are very young. Basically, we're looking at the food chain in reverse."

Then, just as suddenly, I am sad. "I'm going to be here forever, Vinny."

"Isn't that what you want?" he asks.

"Not if I'm just working up to my life as an amoeba..."
"Ahhh, but that's the beauty of it. By then you won't care."

I AM VISUALIZING WITH VINNY, trying to make the throb in my thigh subside.

"I don't think it's working," I say.

"Are you seeing the whole stroke?" he asks. "The comb moving from the top of your leg all the way down to your foot?"

Vinny shuts his own eyes.

"Yeeesss," he purrs. "See the whole stroke of the comb as it takes with it the swelling and pain, the loose fur, the itches... mmmm." He begins to doze off.

"Vinny!" I reprimand him and he jumps awake. "That's a cat thing!"

"OK, all right. We need to find you another image," he concedes.

"Do you think it's infected?" I ask him.

"It's much better," he says, avoiding the actual question. "It will be helpful if you don't dwell on the negative. Now, what image do you want to use? Something that will take away the pressure."

"A huge sponge," I say.

"A sponge? You prefer a sponge to a deep combing?" He is incredulous.

"It's my image," I snap.

"Fine, sponge it is. Now wrap the sponge around your leg and imagine it soaking up the pain."

Vinny begins to purr. With my eyes closed, I feel him walking around me on the bed. He lets go a soft mew. Another set of paws begins to pace the bed. Then softly I feel paws on my thigh, moving slowly up and down. I lift my head to see who it is. Sophie is moving gracefully along my thigh in a series of intricate moves. Vinny turns to me.

"She possesses some extraordinary healing powers," he says, and suddenly I yelp as a sharp pain explodes near my knee.

"Careful of the claws, Sophie," Vinny says. Sophie mews what I take to be an apology and then the sharp pain disappears. I close my eyes again, think of the sponge. The ache begins to fade.

From my half-sleep I speak. "I wasn't sure I would ever see you again," I say.

"You handled yourself very well out there," Vinny tells me.

"What did you two do while I was gone?" I ask him.

"Well...we slept quite a bit, ate. Sophie created a new dance, a study in confinement, quite good really but of course it's hard to see, very small." Then he adds, "Played some cards."

I am leaning closer and closer toward sleep, falling in and out of our conversation.

"Go fish?" I ask.

"Shed poker," he answers, and then I hear only his purr.

I AM GROWING RESTLESS, unable to move from my bed. There are bangs and thuds coming from the kitchen, an enormous racket.

"What's going on?" I yell.

Vinny appears from around the doorway. His black coat is dusted white and there are large clumps of something sticky up and down his legs.

"What are you doing?!" I demand.

"Supervising," he says, a strained fatigue in his voice, "and it's not easy. I do look forward to your full recuperation."

"Supervising what?" I snap.

"Well...Sophie thought it would be nice to have some snacks prepared for our visitor and I thought it might keep the two of them occupied so that you could rest," he answers.

I realize that I have just awoken from an exceptionally long nap. Since returning to full consciousness, I have only been able to sleep little bits at a time. I had attributed my fitfulness to pain but now see that the rambunctious play of a dancing cat and a deeply stupid bear has been more disruptive than I thought.

"Thank you, Vinny," I finally say. "I had a very nice nap. I think I'm feeling better."

"That's good," he says. "Why don't you try to get some more sleep."

"What are you making?" I ask.

"Pigs in a blanket," he tells me.

"What do you have all over you?"

"Blanket."

"But I thought you were supervising."

"With those two it's a sort of paws-on situation."

I can see the exhaustion in his eyes. My journey and sickness have taken their toll on the boy.

"Come sit for a little while, Vinny," I say. "You look tired."

At that moment, a large piece of dough sails through the air. Sophie immediately follows with a screeching meow, Simon enters next, running full tilt from the kitchen.

"Knock it off!" shouts Vinny.

"Behave yourselves!" I add.

Sophie and Simon halt in their tracks and stare at us. They are both an absolute mess of flour, wet and dry.

"Pick up that dough and get back to the kitchen!" I tell them.

Simon reaches carefully for the dough, which has stuck itself in a dripping clump to the chair by the front door. What he can't scrape off he quickly licks up. He turns and hightails it back to the kitchen. Sophie watches him go, looks at me, at Vinny, then tiptoes back herself.

"Do as Vinny says!" I order.

"Thank you. I appreciate your support," Vinny says, and

he wearily turns around, heading for the kitchen to resume his duty.

Left to myself, I manage to prop my head up with an extra pillow. From my perch, I can see through the window. The dot is very near. This is the first time my brain has not been woozy with pain since returning from my journey. As I watch the dot moving ever so slowly toward me, I remember Vinny saying that the visitor would bring us all that we need. I don't believe that that is possible now, not with this new emptiness I'm feeling, worse than ever. I wonder if I have made a great miscalculation. I ventured out into the snow and purged from myself what little definition I knew. For better or for worse, those were the things of me, the stuff I could identify. Now I don't recognize anything, I don't see anything at all. Just a hollowness that dwells inside every bit of me.

I lie in my bed and wish; don't leave me here, don't let the journey be complete.

THE STENCH OF BURNT PIGS IN A BLANKET hangs in the air. We have just finished a meal of canned vegetables and Spam. We had a victorious moment earlier in the day when we were able to instruct Simon to bring cans and a can opener to me for opening. Then came the careful walk back to the kitchen, every step a potential spill. In the end, with a careful line of instruction, we made ourselves a full and nutritious meal.

Vinny sits next to me, glad to be second in command if only for this evening. I have traveled miles in my recovery and am actually feeling cheerful. We are all bristled with excitement as we know the visitor will arrive by morning. In my enthusiasm, I suggest a game of charades.

"I am not a great lover of games," responds Vinny.

"Come on, Vin," I say, "it'll be fun."

"I was thinking more along the lines of a quiet cup of tea in front of the fire."

"Please?" I beg.

"Oohhhh," he whines, "I've been playing games with Sophie and Simon for what feels like months!"

"Go fish!" shouts Simon.

Vinny eyes squint in pain and he lays a paw across his head.

"This will be better," I promise him, "we'll all play."

"If you wish," he moans.

"Charades!" I announce, and Sophie leaps straight up into the air. Simon rocks back and forth, all paws clasped together in excitement.

"What is charades?" the bear asks.

"Just watch for a few minutes, Simon," I say, "then we'll explain it to you."

"Good luck!" Vinny mumbles.

"Who wants to go first?" I ask. Sophie jumps to the center of the bed.

"OK," I say, "Sophie."

Without a moment's hesitation, she begins with a wild series of gestures, a whirling dervish of fur, claws, and teeth. I am stumped but yell out guesses anyway.

"Frantic! Panic! Killer!"

She suddenly stands quietly, only gentle swishes of her tail mark movement. Then her head sways along with a series of ear flicks.

"Ummmm . . . ," I say, "the calm before the storm! Vinny, help me."

She progresses to another group of moves, a low stalking walk that ends in a full collapse.

"The lion sleeps tonight!" I shout, sure that I am right but her gestures continue. I hear Vinny sigh.

"What? What is it, Vinny?"

"She's dancing. She's just dancing. She doesn't know how to play charades," he says. I stop and look at him.

"Well, explain it to her."

Vinny lets out a grunt and heads toward Sophie. They sit

side by side. I turn to begin instructions to Simon. Staring into the dimly lit face of the bear, I feel at a loss as to how to convey the concept. I turn back to the cats, hoping to take some tips from Vinny. They sit quietly together, seemingly silent, both looking toward the fire. I wonder at their communication, envy it. An understanding that encompasses all the senses. It occurs to me that they must know each other very well, deeply and completely, in a way that I have never known anyone. My envy segues to sadness as I return to my huge pupil.

"The goal of the game is to get someone to guess your answer without you saying anything."

I look at him to gauge my progress. It seems hopeless.

"You have to express yourself completely through your body"—and suddenly, with that explanation, it seems odd to me that I was the one who suggested this game. Simon stares at me, expectantly, as if I have not yet begun the instruction.

"Just watch a few more rounds, Simon, I think that's the best way for you to learn." I sneak a peak at Vinny, hoping he didn't hear my admission of defeat.

"We're ready," I say, and the cats turn to face us.

"Sophie's prepared to try again," Vinny announces.

I nod and we return to our original positions. Sophie moves to the center of the bed and sits, perfect statue form. She does not move.

"Statue!" I shout.

"Wait," says Vinny, and he turns to Sophie and meows.

She responds with a little hop up and an arch of her back. She then holds her tail erectly up in the air and uses it to slash the air several times. I look at Vinny.

"Is this a clue?" I ask, and he turns to Sophie, flicks his ear and she repeats the movement.

I turn to Vinny again and shake my head.

"Six words," he tells me, clearly disappointed in my failure to guess correctly. He signals Sophie to begin. She flicks her tail once.

"First word," I say, and Vinny nods approval.

Sophie returns to her statuesque pose.

"Still!" I guess. But she doesn't move. "Frozen! Stone. Dead."

Vinny is looking at me in the same sort of tired way I often see him look at Simon.

"I'm not being stupid," I snap at him, "but you're not helping."

"It's quite obvious," he says. "What is she?"

"That's what I'm trying to figure out!" I am aggravated by his condescension.

"She's sitting there, doing nothing. She's a—" Vinny stops, holding out his paw, hoping that I will fill in the blank. He repeats himself, "She's a—," again with the paw outreached as if the answer is clear as a bell.

I am feeling very stupid as I stare at him, mute.

"Cat!" Vinny finally explodes. "Cat! She's a"—paw extended—"cat!"

"Well, I know she's a cat but—" and I stop myself. "Oh, 'cat,' " I say, shocked at missing such an obvious clue. "OK, first word—Cat."

"*Cat on a Hot Tin Roof,*" says Simon with an unusually cool edge in his voice.

His tone is jarring. Every pair of eyes turns to him, all wide, all stunned. His gaze is blank and straight ahead, disengaged. His brightness faded, gone as quickly as it came.

Sophie mews and jumps down off the bed, done with the game.

"Is there dessert?" Simon asks.

I turn to Vinny, hoping he can explain to me what just transpired. He simply shakes his head. I can't tell if he is wondering at Simon or disapproving of me. He jumps down off the bed.

"I'll knock some cookies off the shelf for dessert if that's all right with you," says Vinny.

I nod and then I am left alone. Cat, I think. There could be no other answer. She is nothing but a cat, simply a cat. I am lingering inside this idea when I realize that I am feeling deep green envy. I want to be the one who is sitting completely still before a guessing crowd. I want to hear the obvious answer to me. But in my head I hear a litany of answers, none more right than the next, certainly nothing as right as "cat."

Then Simon's eerie tone rings in my ears. I am unsettled, my brain flashing on pictures of my first terrifying encounter with the bear, his all-knowing evil.

Then I begin to understand what I know. It is not my anger that fuels this bear, it is my fear. My fear of not knowing; why I can't wear pants to school, why the boys always rule, what it is to be a girl; my fear of not knowing what Sophie's gesture meant; my fear of not knowing what mine would mean. And, of course, my fear of not knowing what is inside me now, my even greater fear of finding out, and, worst of all, knowing that whatever it is, I will have to accept it or all of this will have been for naught.

All of it turns to Simon's advantage and can only defeat me.

THERE IS A KNOCK AT THE DOOR that breaks my sleep. We all stir toward wake. Sun spikes the windows, it is morning. The knock comes again.

"Answer it, Simon," grumbles Vinny.

Simon staggers toward the door, big bear sleep still in his eyes. "I'm so tired I could hibernate."

We are all focused on the door, each of us realizing in our own time that this is the visitor, finally arrived. Simon reaches for the handle, turns it, and opens the door.

There stands a woman, at her feet, two cats.

IT SEEMS LIKE HOURS before anyone speaks or moves. Then without a word, the woman enters the cabin, cats at her heels. I am struck with the notion that I have met this woman before. I watch her closely. She seems unaffected by the notion of a bear answering our door, moving with a determined confidence, an assumption that she is welcomed.

She's a big woman, though it's hard to determine how much of her is actually just layers of sweater and coat. I try to pin down what is familiar. Her head is nearly covered with a rainbow of wool scarves that have caught up shoots of blond curls in their wrapped weave. She stands tall and as she walks, I see an awkward hitch in her gait. But mostly it is her face that draws me in.

It is the palest palette I have ever seen. Drawn on it, two perfect circles of rose blush and two deep dark eyes. Her lips are painted with a darker rose, almost red, they outline a tiny mouth that bends away just slightly from a perfect movie star nose. It is a big face with fine features and from where I sit, I am certain that it glows. I do not even think to stop staring. I am puzzled and dumbstruck.

In her trail stride the cats, one behind the next. They have walked in from the cold and snow wearing nothing but their fur. The lead cat is a full-bodied creature who moves with a swagger, and as I study him, there is something familiar, too, in him. He has a thick coat of tiger-stripe gray fur and a bold face on a strong head. His paws are marked with white spats. Behind him stands a little orange cat who I immediately mistake for Sophie. Only when I finally pull my eyes off this trio do I see that Sophie is still hunkered down between my legs, staring herself, a bewilderment pasted across her whole being. Vinny sits unfettered, looking formally attired for the meeting, in his standard black with white accents. Simon, having eventually shut the door, curls into a ball and returns to his sleep.

"Hi," the woman finally says after removing most of the

scarves from her head. "I hope it's OK, I parked right in front of the door. Didn't want the cats to sink in the snow."

The lead cat nods as if to confirm this commonsense thinking.

I look out the window and filling the whole scene is the side of a bright green pickup truck. I turn back to the woman, continue to stare. Vinny clears his throat. "Of course, that's fine—and welcome. We've been looking forward to your visit for some time now." He moves a front paw toward my foot and whacks me through the covers, urging me to speak.

"Yes," I say. He whacks me again. "Yes," I repeat.

"Simon!" Vinny says, and the bear jerks. "Take our guest's overcoats." The bear stumbles to his feet, groggy and swaying. He picks up the pile of sweaters and coats at the woman's feet.

"Take them where?" Simon asks.

"Closet," Vinny says under his breath.

Sophie begins to stretch upward, cautiously extending a paw in the direction of the newcomers. She wants a better view. Simon has thrown his bundle into the closet and shut the door. He leans against the wall and slides down into a sitting position.

"We played charades last night," Simon offers.

The woman turns toward him. There is a silence and then the bear adds, "The girl got angry and I won."

"Congratulations," the woman says to him.

Her kindness toward Simon impresses me. She turns back in my direction.

"Are you ill?" she asks.

I don't know how to answer her. To my thinking, I'm not really ill. But at this moment, to explain what has occurred in the recent past seems difficult at best.

"Mending," I finally say.

"That's better than ill, I guess," she says to me with a smile.

Sophie inches her way toward Vinny and anchors her head just behind his. He turns toward her and then back to the guests.

"Sophie would like to offer you some snacks, if you would like them," Vinny says.

"Sophie?" the woman nods toward my ginger cat as if to confirm her identity.

"I apologize," says Vinny immediately. "We haven't introduced ourselves. I am Vincent the Black Cat. This is Sophie, that's Simon over there in a heap, and this is our girl," he says, gesturing toward me.

"I'm Nellie," the woman says, "and this is Sid"—she points to the tiger-stripe, who nods a greeting. "The little one is Clara."

Clara seems unaware of her introduction as she sniffs the floorboards inch by inch.

"So . . . ," says Vinny, and he steals a glance at me, hoping that I will begin to hold up my end of the conversation burden.

But I am unable to think. I feel mesmerized by the woman and shy in front of her cats. I want to disappear under the blankets. She has such a sure sense of herself, I am certain she sees me, every inch, for the empty fraud that I am.

"Snacks all around then?" asks Vinny, and he hops down off the bed with Sophie at his heels. They exit to the kitchen.

Nellie has finally finished removing her layers of clothing and I see now that she is not as large as I originally thought. "Full-bodied" is the word that comes to mind. She has the curves of a real woman, I think. She walks toward me and my heart pounds. I search her for clues.

"It was a difficult trip," she says, sitting herself on the edge of my bed.

She is so precise in her position that I don't have to move even an inch. As if she can feel exactly my pain, she finds the one spot that will not jar my leg.

"It took you a long time," I say.

She is looking right through me. I'm sure she can see the neurons snapping inside my brain.

"We had a lot of setbacks. The truck broke down for one and then there was a wild blizzard, couldn't see a thing. I don't know how long we had to wait for that to end. Couldn't tell night for day."

"I know what you mean," I answer, and then we stop talking for a bit.

In the silence, she pulls back the blankets and lays a hand on my leg. I expect to jerk with pain but instead a cool wave of calm settles on my thigh. I stare at her hand, hoping the touch will never end.

Her focus moves back to my face, with her hand still resting on my leg, she says, "You've made a real mess here."

"My thigh exploded," I tell her, meeting her steady stare.

I feel like I am crawling inside her face, examining the brown of her eyes from the back of her eyeballs. It dawns on me that from this vantage point I can see the world from her point of view. I look past the brown and there on the other side is me.

"Yes," she says, "I see that."

I am startled, think she has caught me snooping. I jump back to my side of the brown. I have no idea what she is responding to, I am lost as to our conversation so I just nod. Then the quiet comes on us again. Suddenly I want to ask her if she knows where we are, that somehow she might know what has me baffled, this question that is looming larger and larger in my brain. But there is so much else hanging in the air right now. Specificity would diminish the moment.

Her cats sit quietly at her feet. She is clearly the captain of her ship. I envy her authority and wish that I were in charge of my pack, but I know that I have let things get far too out of hand for that ever to be the case.

"Have you been here long?" she asks me.

"I don't really know," I say as I realize I have lost all track of time, "awhile. Vinny wished for you," I tell her unsolicited.

"I know. Sid told me," she nods toward the tiger-stripe and the tiger-stripe nods at me.

There's something aloof about this cat, makes me feel a little like a geek.

"Sid talks?" I ask.

"Oh, yes," she says.

"This talking-cat thing is new for me. Has he always talked?"

"Pretty much," she answers, "haven't you, Sid?"

"Yes," says Sid.

"And Clara?" I ask.

"No," says Sid, "she sings."

"Sophie dances," I tell them, "isn't that funny? So much alike."

"Yes," says Sid, "funny."

The cat is bored by me, I'm certain. Suddenly there is a clamor in the kitchen and then Vinny sticks his head out.

"Simon," he says, "I need you in here, please." The bear obliges and shuffles off.

"Seems like a nice bear," Nellie says.

"Nicer than he used to be," I tell her. Her hand moves slightly on my thigh and I feel a shift in the center of the relief that her touch offers.

From the kitchen, Vinny and Sophie enter, leading Simon, who carries a plate topped with pigs in a blanket. Between the pigs lost to the burnt batches and those that were far too furry to offer a guest, there are only eleven pigs left. But despite the small number, Vinny said, from an etiquette point of view, it was better to offer a little than nothing at all.

Simon, obviously instructed by Vinny, offers the plate to Nellie. She takes a pig and hands it to me. I take it because she offers it. She takes another one for herself and smiles at Simon, who seems to swoon a little in response to her attention. She weakens him, I think, and then I file the information away.

Sid takes the next one but waves Simon off when he sets the plate in front of Clara.

"We'll share this one," he tells Simon.

The bear nods obediently and returns to his more familiar felines. He snatches two off the plate for himself and then sets the remainder in front of Sophie and Vinny, who each claim their own separate pig.

We are settling into our meal when I hear an unusual sound. A haunting melody that floats tenderly through the cabin. I look at Vinny, Sophie, and Simon. We have all heard it. Together we look toward Nellie and Sid and then finally to Clara. The little orange cat is standing tall in a pool of sunlight, singing for her early morning supper.

NELLIE HAS CLEANED MY WOUND and it finally has a proper dressing. With only a day of her attention, the swelling has already decreased.

"It feels much better," I tell her.

I am worried that Vinny might take offense, think that I prefer my new caretaker to him, but when I look for him, I find him lying by the fire, lost in conversation with Sid. I cannot see Sophie from my bed but am certain that she has pulled Clara off to work on a new piece. I think it must be the first time that Sophie has worked with live orchestration.

"You're going to have to start moving a bit," Nellie tells me, "too much more of this lying about and you're likely to develop pneumonia."

I cannot imagine even shifting my leg but I know that if Nellie tells me to do it, I will. Simon has begun to growl softly in his sleep.

"Today you will just sit up," she says, and I nod.

She sets about preparing a chair and I understand now that she intends to actually get me from my bed. My first instinct is to call for Vinny, have him intervene. But Nellie moves with such determined force that I am rendered powerless. Without my own consent, I begin to prop myself up in preparation for the move.

"Good," I hear her say, "we'll do this in stages."

She takes another pillow from the couch and with a grasp on my arm and a hand on my back, she pulls me fully upright. Then she adjusts all the pillows so that they hold me snugly in my new position. Under her supervision, my fear disappears and Simon returns to his quiet slumber.

As she turns to focus on the chair, my head fills with cotton. I feel queasy and the room seems to rock.

"You'll be fine," she says without even looking at me. "You just have to regain your equilibrium."

Immediately the pitching in my stomach settles.

"Simon?" she calls, and the bear wakes faster and more completely than I have ever before seen.

He hops to his feet with deeply uncharacteristic quickness. He rushes to her but seems to shy away when he reaches her. His gaze hits the floor and his claws interlock with each other, he shuffles his bear feet. I am certain that if a bear could blush, Simon would be beet red. Vinny has joined me on the bed, seated at my side. He watches the bear.

"I believe that old Simon has developed a crush," Vinny says quietly under his breath.

"Yes, Nellie," Simon says.

"I need your help with something," she says gently, seeming to understand his vulnerable standing.

"Yes," he says.

Vinny chuckles out loud, then tries to cover himself with a quick clearing of his throat. Simon's head snaps in our direction, he looks directly at Vinny.

"Fur ball," Vinny says quickly, "not to worry, I'm fine."

I look toward Sid, ready to throw him a knowing glance, make him understand that I am not the dunce I immediately proved myself to be upon his arrival. But Sid is not even watching, he is focused on the fire. He has no interest in our tiny little lives.

"I want to get the wheels off the legs of the bed," she explains to Simon, "and I need you to lift the frame so that I can do that."

Simon immediately moves toward the bed, prepared, I fear, to capsize the whole thing, me included.

"Hold on, Simon"—Nellie is patient—"be very careful; slow and gentle."

Simon nods and finishes his cross to the bed on tiptoes.

"One corner at a time, Simon, and just lift it a tiny little bit," she instructs.

Simon is so careful that I barely feel the movement as each corner is raised and the casters are removed.

"Thank you, Simon," Nellie says when the job is done. "You've been an enormous help."

"Yes," says Simon.

Vinny shakes his head. I fear he's going to make fun of my bear. I knock him with my elbow before he makes a sound.

"I didn't say a word," he mutters.

Nellie turns the chair upside down and I understand that she is creating for me a wheelchair. Using twine, she secures a caster on each leg. She flips the chair back over and tests her creation with a swift push that sends it sailing across the room.

"Impressive," says Vinny, and then he looks toward me. "That's just the sort of thing our girl would think of."

Nellie gives a smile and nods. She proceeds to ready the chair with padding and blankets.

"This is good," says Vinny, "it's time you were up."

We both watch with admiration as Nellie creates my new mode of transportation. It occurs to me that Vinny is right. I would have come up with this notion were I not befuddled with pain and distracted by questions of the most basic natures. Though it is Nellie I am watching construct the chair, I start to feel an undeserved sense of pride in my own ingenuity.

"Vincent," Sid suddenly says.

"Yes, Sid."

"I'm not at all sure that you are right."

"In what regard, Sid?" Vinny's tone is different than I know, it is that of an academician, a coffeehouse debater.

"Kafka was an absurdist," Sid continues.

"Agreed," says Vinny as he moves toward the edge of the bed.

"You cannot apply the 'Man against Nature' thematic theory to his work"—Sid is making quote marks in the air with his paws—"or 'Man against anything,' for that matter. He simply was not working in that realm."

"The realm of his work is irrelevant," says Vinny. He turns back to me. "I'll be back in a bit," he says, and then jumps down to rejoin his new best friend by the fire.

I turn my attention to Nellie and feel a shift toward a brand-new balance.

NELLIE HAS ENORMOUS STRENGTH. She lifts me with a graceful ease as if she is lifting a pound of sugar. But even with the calming effect she has on me, the spiking slam of pain that crushes down on my leg as it hangs below my body makes me nearly black out.

I am seated in the chair, covered in blankets, and still I shout in anguish. My head falls forward, the pain drops a notch in intensity, and I realize I have stopped shouting. It is not me that is creating the deafening roar. It is Simon.

I lift my eyes and see the huge white bear rearing up on his hind legs. A terrifying sight, he slashes the air with furious paws. His eyes have gone yellow.

Nellie turns to me and forces me to meet her, eye to eye. She knows, I think. She knows my connection to the bear and understands that only I can reign him in.

But I'm not angry, I think. Then I remember my fear. The true base of my bear's power. In a lightning-fast journey, I travel the paths of my brain to the place where fear lives. It's tucked behind pain, it's covered in anger. Weaved together with darkness, it rests comfortably beneath everything I know, intermingled with everything I don't. Tough to see, but the path stops here. Then I sense a true feeling, I don't know if this pain will ever stop. I latch on to this concept and hurry back along the path, dragging the fear, kicking and screaming, forward. Simon is losing steam. Nellie and I remain with eyes locked.

"I'm afraid it will never end," I say out loud, and Simon settles down onto all fours, falls back on his rump, and looks about blankly.

Nellie and I are still locked together, a single force, when I scream inside her head, "WHERE ARE WE?!"

Before I can hear the answer I'm hoping she has, we pull back from each other, reestablishing our boundaries. We pass through an odd moment and settle back into our places.

"The pain will pass," says Nellie finally, "and in the meantime, you'll learn a thing or two. Now, how about a change of scenery?"

I nod and she wheels me toward the window, sunshine falling over me like a blanket of spring.

MOST OF THE MORNING HAS PASSED with the two of us, side by side, staring out the window. We've propped my leg up on a table and with the recent weird trauma passed, I am feeling serenely contented, quietly jubilant to be out of the bed.

It's a pristine day and it sets my mind free to wander. I remember my first days in this cabin, the swirling snow, the

wind whipping around the corners of the house, the anxiousness I felt as I watched out this window, images flying by.
Pictures of the sickness trapped in my thigh. Visions of my
battle out in the cold. I want to revel in the magnitude of what
I have survived. With wide eyes, I take in the expanse outside
my window. It is clear, only vibrant blue sky and sparkling
white snow. I give myself the moment, relax into the glory of
it all.

"Feeling better, aren't you," Nellie says just as I am about
to announce how much better I'm feeling.

I shift my eyes in her direction, hoping to catch some new
clue. But she offers up nothing, simply stares ahead, rocking
slowly, so I just nod my head in confirmation.

"If it were up to me," I finally say, "I would stay in this
moment forever."

Nellie lets out a soft laugh.

"There's nothing sweeter than the moment after survival.
Not a care in the world," she says. "Enjoy it because, un-
fortunately, a moment will only last a moment. That's what
they do."

A gust kicks up against the house and a funnel of crystallized snow spins by the window. In the sparkling of the crys-
tals, I see the questions that remain unanswered and in a sense
they are the whole journey. Without their answers, it will all
count for nothing.

"What's your deepest fear?" she asks.

I smile and shake my head.

"What?" she asks me.

"You're a funny duck," I say, and she tilts her head, sug-
gesting that I've made an irrelevant point.

"So?" she asks, wanting an answer to her question.

"That I don't know how to love."

My response surprises me and all I can do is let it sit there,
wonder at it.

"Me, too," she says without missing a beat.

"Really?" I can't believe she thinks that. It appears to me that Nellie knows how to do everything.

"Absolutely," she continues, "don't trust myself for a second."

"I would say you're an unusually loving person," I tell her, again taken slightly aback by my own statement.

Nellie looks at me with genuine alarm.

"Of course, you're no Sophie," I add glibly, feeling compelled to qualify myself, protect myself. The moment is too intense. Then I am disappointed that I didn't let the fact remain.

"Why do you think you don't know how to love?" she asks me.

"I don't know" is all that I say and again I am deeply disappointed in myself.

"You must know something," she says, "you were quick enough to give me an answer."

"Nothing lasts," I say with my focus out the window.

The wind has picked up and my moment of clarity is gone. The pictures are returning; pictures of Joe and Johnny and Ray, the ones that I thought I had loved.

"Every time," I continue, "I'm sure it looks different. I think, 'This time it's real,' and every time it dies. And it happens somewhere deep inside me, so deep that I can't reach it, can't change it back."

I turn to look at Nellie and am unsurprised to see her mouthing my words as I speak.

"And when it's gone," I say, "it's gone. And it's got nothing to do with what I wanted, with what I had hoped for, or what I had planned. It just goes."

"Yup," says Nellie, and nothing more.

"Somehow, I went from being Ungirl to Slutgirl to Frigidgirl," I say, suddenly awash in the stories that sprang from my leg, "and I don't know how."

"Wait a minute," Nellie says, "are we talking about love or sex?"

"Intimacy," I say.

"Aaahhh," she responds with a smile. Then she says, "Do you think that, once upon a time, long, long ago, men and women actually trusted each other?"

"You forgot 'in a faraway land,' " I tell her.

"Yeah," she says, "Eden."

"Very cynical, Nellie. I'm not sure that's helpful."

"Oh, we're both full of shit and you know it," she says, then, "You should have seen what I did to my husband."

"You should have seen what I did to MY husband!" I state.

This makes her laugh and then I can't stand another moment.

"Have we met before? Do we know each other?" I ask her, demand her.

"You're the only person I've ever known," she says to me, completely guileless.

Her answer annoys me. I'm about to ask her what kind of downtown, esoteric hooey is that when Vinny makes his presence known with a short cough.

"Excuse me." He is standing at the base of my chair. "I, perhaps more than anyone, am absolutely delighted that the two of you have found in each other such a profound and stimulating connection." He looks to Sid, who nods. "However, I think I speak for the rest of us when I say that we are long overdue for lunch."

He turns away and pads off toward the kitchen, never looking back, confident that Nellie will follow, which she does. He disappears around the corner and only a disgusted muttering about can openers and thumbs remains in the air.

"Wait. Nellie?" I have to stop her only because as she walks farther away from me, my need for her intensifies.

"What is it?" she asks me, but I can't find words.

"I think emptiness equals sadness, don't you?" she says.

She has found my words for me and, in return, I want to answer her for real. "I've recently purged myself of most of what I've always known and now it seems there's nothing left."

"As if you've forgotten your life?"

"No, it's not that..."

Vinny's face pops out from around the corner of the kitchen door. He stares, waiting. Clara has appeared and rubs against Nellie's leg. She bends to pick up the cat, who automatically swats her hand and quickly darts away only to return when Nellie stands upright.

"You ever notice how happy they are to stay and be sweet as long as you don't try to hold on to them?" Nellie asks me with a smile.

Memories on which I have built myself, now excavated, they mingle like single girls at a cocktail party. The space in which they were once contained sits waiting, so void that I think it's creating a vacuum effect, stealing even my tears.

I AM SITTING ON THE COUCH. I want to only sit up now. I never want to lie down again. Nellie is beside me and on either armrest sit Vinny and Sid. Simon is rolling around on the floor, trying to catch his stubby tail. We await the debut of Sophie and Clara in concert.

"Will it be soon?" I ask Vinny.

"I was told eight P.M. sharp, but obviously there has been a delay," he says.

"Do you think they need help?" Nellie asks.

"We have been, in no uncertain terms, advised to steer clear of the creative process," says Sid.

I look at Sid and smile. It's the first time he's spoken to me without a condescending tone or exhausted sigh. I feel like I just got an excellent report card.

"Well, they've been working very hard," Nellie says.

I realize that though it's been only two days since the arrival of our guests, the changes in my little family have been profound. My thoughts are filled with Nellie now. I have barely seen Sophie at all and Vinny speaks at length only to Sid. My conversations with him are merely in passing. The thought makes me sad but something in it also rings of rightness.

"I'll do it," says Vinny, who prepares to jump to the floor. "I'll see what the problem is."

But at that moment, from around the door of the bathroom, creep two orange kittenlike cats. I stare for several moments in an attempt to determine which is Sophie. Only when they assume their positions and Sophie is clearly center stage do I know which is mine. Clara has leapt up onto a small wooden crate that sits off to one side. The two look at each other, blink in slow motion, and then Clara's tiny mouth opens and a clear round tone comes forth. It floats up into the air and envelops the cabin. It moves silently, making only its singular rich sound. So piercing and so correct it is that tears come immediately to my eyes.

Sophie has barely moved. Her dance is solemn and slow. As Clara's tone begins to move to a higher and even more mournful note, Sophie fills the space with sweeping gentle movements. There are no breaks between ground and air, between forward and back. She is one long, flowing gesture, leaving room for the sound to dance around her.

It is at this moment that I understand that Sophie has changed, her dance is different. The dramatic leaps and grand spins of her earlier work have given way to a simpler and softer movement. She is now one of two and offers up what lives between them. Clara's voice moves from one note to the next, always with a heartbreaking resonance that feels as though it comes more from inside me than from out. Sophie floats, fully extended, riding the song.

Nellie's weight shifts toward me. Vinny's face is running

tears. Simon sits with slackened jaw and Sid stares with a hurt that I cannot begin to know. We watch the two orange cats. They are many lifetimes ahead of us all. We watch with a longing to be further along than we are.

There is silence in their song and a stillness in their dance. Together, they make peace.

NELLIE AND I HAVE BEEN TALKING ALL DAY. She wheeled me into the kitchen this morning and we have been here since, making a celebration feast.

Nellie says I deserve to be saluted for my heroic mission, my courage in the face of deep scariness. With a nod of approval from Vinny and even Sid, I accepted the offer.

The cabin is buzzing with activity. We are all very excited about the dinner. Simon has been bringing in wood all morning. Truth be told, he's brought in far too much and we would like him to stop. But he is so smitten with Nellie, wants so much to please her, that we are afraid he will be crushed if we ask him to stop. Sophie and Clara have been assigned to the decorations and are, at present, shredding an old sheet that is to be our tablecloth. Vinny says that it is a fine art and that the sheet will be a very valuable textile when they are done with it. Vinny and Sid are in their usual spots, in front of the fire. I'm told they are preparing their toasts.

Nellie has set the menu and I am the assistant, peeling or slicing whatever is set in front of me. She has found things in this kitchen that I never knew existed, the potatoes that I am peeling, for example.

"I think you have magical powers," I say to Nellie.

"Hardly," she snorts.

"Where did you find fresh vegetables and a roast?" I ask like I'm trying to trick her into a confirmation of her witchery.

"I wished we had them. Then I opened the refrigerator and there they were."

If I hadn't had the same experience myself, I might not have believed her but I remember wishing for a hot bath. I remember wishing for Spam. I remember Vinny wishing for her.

Nellie handles herself in the kitchen like a great chef. She works on several things at once, balancing simmering creams with basting juices with flipping crepes.

"Where did you learn all this?" I ask her.

"I don't know. Here and there."

"What can't you do?"

"I told you. Love," she states with her usual forthrightness.

"I don't know if I believe you," I say.

"And why should you? When it comes to love I'm not trustworthy. I never follow through on what I promise."

My heart is sinking. I'm desperate for Nellie to have the answers. Though I'm not sure who or what she is, in my gut I think she is extraordinary. I am convinced that if she can't love, then I will never learn how. It seems like two sides of the same coin.

"Well, what about your husband?" I ask, determined to prove her wrong. "Didn't you love him?"

"No," she says, "but I wanted to."

"You didn't love him at all." My question is a statement.

"I loved him, but not in that way," she concedes. "We didn't have sex for months at a time."

"Well, why did you marry him?" My tone is indignant but I know the response better myself than anyone else could ever say.

"I had lost hope," she says as she stirs a bubbling sauce.

I'm instantly bored with her response, tired of the same old answer. Then I realize that I have never heard her answer before.

"I don't know," she continues, "I guess I figured that if I was just going to keep falling in love only to find out that I wasn't in love, then I might as well just stay where I was, take what was good about it, and accept the rest. He was a good person."

"How long did it last?"

"About a minute and a half," she says with a beaten smile.

I try to muster up some compassion to replace the agitation that is rising up in me. I attribute my response to the uncanny similarities in our stories. That is, I figure, how I know that I am not getting the real answers. It's also how I know that Nellie doesn't even know it. I swallow hard, holding back, I don't want to throw it in her face. I don't want to challenge her. That will break the spell. I'm sure I'm sitting silently and then I hear myself talking.

"I wanted a wedding" is what I hear.

I look at Nellie. She is turning to me, a stunned expression on her face. For a split second I think it is she who has said it, but then I gasp out loud and I know that the confession came from me. Nellie spins back to the stove, takes a smoking saucepan off the burner.

That's when I find myself on the other side of her eyes again. This hasn't happened since the day she arrived. I watch the cream in the saucepan fall away from its boil. As if I'm inside a camera lens, I watch the counter slide by, the kitchen floor, the wooden leg up to the top of the table. Then I watch me speak.

"I did," I say, "I wanted a wedding before I was too old to be a picture-perfect bride and it seemed like Ray was probably my last best shot at that. I wanted to be the reason for the bittersweet tears. I wanted to be demure grace swept across the threshold. I wanted to be the beautiful part of the beautiful young couple. Fresh and pure and sweet. I wanted to be the girl."

Now it seems I see the scene from both sides; I sit at the table, peeler resting in my hand. I stare at the grain of the wood on the floor. I am shocked at my words and sick at the truth that rings around them. I expect to hear reproach in Nellie's response, condemnation for my supremely deep shallowness.

Instead, she asks quietly, "Did it work?"

"I looked pretty good in the dress but I'd say that's as far as I got."

There is no movement in the kitchen, not a sound until I set the peeler down and look straight at Nellie. I am fully back on my side now, feeling my emptiness so acutely that I am forced to realize that for that split second when I sat on the other side of Nellie's eyes, it had disappeared.

"God!" I utter in a whispered shout. "I'm pathetic!"

There are tears in my eyes. There are tears in hers. Between us, a path alive with connection. It feels like this moment could spin off in a thousand different directions and then we both begin to laugh, quietly at first and then growing into wild peals of hysterics. We pound the table and kick at the floor in complete unison. Then we begin to wind down, ending back at a silence as we grope for air, brush away tears.

I take a deep breath and start back on the cucumbers. Nellie turns to the counter. She prepares the meat for the oven, tying string around a roast, something I've never understood.

"It's not pathetic," she finally says, "it's just too bad. Seems like there ought to be more ways than that to feel like a girl."

Her statement is simple but it runs in circles around my brain, won't settle into a crevice.

"I'm smarter than this," I say, "and much further along."

"Yeah, right," she says.

"Listen to us," I whine, "it sounds like we're about to decide that we should get really radical and burn our bras."

"Well, that's not going to help," she says, throwing the potatoes, onions, and carrots into the roasting pan. "Bras are a girl thing. They go with tits. If we intend to feel like girls, we're going to need our bras."

I shake my head, rest my forehead on my hand. This is complicated stuff. Being a girl has so many different voices and so few opportunities to use them. Then I slam the table with an open hand.

"Hey!" I yelp. "I got an idea."

Nellie turns to me, having just put the roast in the oven. "Yes?"

"Let's feel like girls because we are!"

"Whhooaa!" she says. "That's deep."

Then she throws her head back in mock exhaustion. "I gotta sit down," and she does.

"I WAS REALLY YOUNG," Nellie says as she begins to tell me about her first love.

"How young?" I ask.

"Seventeen."

"Me, too. And do you think you loved him?" I can't give up the hope that Nellie will give me my answer.

"Well, that's what pisses me off. I've never been able to figure that one out and it has always felt like if I could, everything else might stand a chance," she says. I nod.

"He was much older," she continues, "twice my age actually and he spoke with a wonderful accent that made me feel full grown and really sexy ..." There's a half-smirk on her face as she trails off. I click off another point on our ever-increasing list of things in common. "How in the hell are you supposed to know if you're in love when it's the first time?"

"All you can do is match it against what you've seen," I tell her, "like DNA testing."

"Exactly! And when there is no case study for comparison?" she asks me.

There's an idea simmering in my brain having to do with learning about love from watching your parents. But before I can express it, I am thinking about learning about a lack of love from watching your parents. Then I am thinking about divorce rates and then my brain is filled with millions and millions of grown children who are trying to live peaceably in bodies and brains that are a combination of two people who could not live peaceably.

"There is not any more wood outside," Simon announces, barreling through the kitchen door.

I look down, not wanting to deal with the bear. Nellie rises and extends her hand toward Simon. He shyly lifts his paw, eyes glistening with anticipation. Nellie takes his paw in both her hands.

"Thank you, Simon," she says. "I don't know what we would have done without you."

She sounds so sincere that I start to feel a certain amount of pride on behalf of my bear.

"You are welcome," he says.

"I think you ought to take a break now," she says.

"No," he says.

"OK, then"—without missing a beat—"would you clear the snow off the truck? I don't want it to get buried."

He gallops out of the kitchen.

"Are you going somewhere?" I ask her, immediately upset at the notion of being without her.

"No. But did you want a big dim bear staring at you for the rest of the afternoon? Now, where were we?" she mutters, and she pulls her chair up to the table.

We sit across from each other, our cups of tea touching.

"You were trying to figure out if you loved your first love."

Vinny and Sid enter the kitchen, walking in unison, side by side. Their heads are lowered as if deep in conversation. Sid jumps up on the counter, bats open a cupboard door, and pushes a small bag of crunchies onto the floor. Vinny picks up the bag in his mouth as Sid jumps back down and rejoins Vinny at his side. They turn and exit back out to the living room. Nellie and I sit unacknowledged, watching the cats and then an empty doorway.

"I suddenly feel disregarded," says Nellie.

"Continue," I say, and turn back to her.

I take a full look at her sitting at the table. She wears pants and settles deep into the chair, her legs wide open. She sits like a boy, I think. Then I see myself on the first day of fourth grade, having no idea how to sit in pants, no sense of how open is too open. Why did we keep our legs together anyway? Because we were girls or because we wore dresses? I'm wondering if I've just come upon a clue when Nellie speaks.

"I was in love with him" is what she says.

"And did you love him?"

"Yes. It must have been that, I had no reason to lie at that point, no way of lying. I would not have known how. I had nothing to lose, nothing to prove. I was pure."

"And you felt sexy, you said that," I say, trying to cover all the bases, maybe prove that she was normal, at least back then.

"Yeah, for the very first time ever. It was like a drug, feeling that way."

"So what happened?" I hang on every word, waiting to be vindicated, hearing my story told with new evidence.

"He was mesmerized by me. I was some sort of redeeming angel to him. Young, alive, sweet, fresh. He worshiped me and I blossomed in the midst of all of it. I never ever once had the thought that it could end, that it would be possible for him to ever feel another way. It was like an age-old romance, I knew he couldn't live without me."

Nellie is deep inside her perfect love story that could have happened hundreds of years ago. She could have been a lady, he could have been a king. I am on the edge of my seat.

"Then there came a day," she says, and I can hear that the disbelief still lives with her, "I started to feel sick inside. Trapped. Suffocated. Swallowed up. I felt freakish, all wrong. This classic love had gone too far, been too much. This is not what I need, I remember thinking, and it didn't make sense. I needed to be lighter than this, freer than this. I needed to be relieved. So I wrote him a letter and told him so and then I was."

We are both quiet as we relive the devastation of letting go and being let go so easily. It should have taken great battles, plagues, and natural disasters. Continents should have shifted. That's the age-old story. But it only took a letter.

"And the funny thing is, I still look back on it and think, 'That looks like a great love story.' " Nellie is barely there, like a confusing memory.

How open is too open? The question is sounding in my head. I am annoyed to find myself still thinking about fourth grade and pants. How open is too open? Then I am not thinking about fourth grade. I am thinking of me at seventeen; a dress-girl wide open like a pants-girl.

"Nellie!" I shout. I am nearly standing.

"We only changed our clothes! We never changed the rest of us." There's a sound of victory in my voice.

For a split second I think I have new evidence, grounds for a retrial. We are innocent, we have to be, I think. We only grew up and tried to love. How could that make us guilty? She said it herself, it was an age-old romance, an age-old romance, and she was brand-new. It was a fair reaction, not a condemnation to never knowing love.

"I don't think I believe in forever," she says, disconnected. "I see no evidence."

"You *were* trapped," I say, and then fall silent.

"I didn't really want him gone, not all the way," she continues, having heard nothing of my catharsis, "and, in fact, we did come together many more times over the next several years but I was tougher, glibber. I needed my own place in the world. My actions had justified his wandering eye, his inconsistent attention. Then, he married someone else."

She stops talking but I know what is next. I don't need her to finish. I am pulled back into the pain, the dull and constant ache, the first understanding of hopelessness. The discovery that falling asleep is the easy part, it is waking that hurts more than anything else, when every single morning is about having to remember that the perfect love didn't survive. And all the perfect loves that have followed march across my mind; each a flawless picture, each extinct.

"If that's not love, what is?" I finally say with a complete lack of conviction, exhausted.

"I don't know," Nellie says. There is a gentle smile on her lips as she adds, "I told you that."

We are swimming in a sea of excuses, I think, having laid the corpses of our failed loves gently upon the shoulders of social change, physiological mutation, generational decay. All of it true and yet the truth has not yet been revealed. Somewhere in the midst of all of this, I know that we are responsible for our own hearts. And we must pry them open again and again, regardless of the pain or the fear, until finally we will change; like losing a tail or gaining a thumb.

"Regardless," I say, and nothing more.

It's clear that Nellie has listened to my thoughts. I see a ray of light break across her face, like a rock pick having broken away the tiniest of pebbles from our cave dwelling and day is just on the other side. We are on the threshold of finally breathing fresh air.

"Oh, oh, oh"—my head is shaking back and forth—"the pictures are all wrong. Scrap that DNA theory. We've got nothing for comparison."

I sit across from her, feeling remarkably alone, but I begin to also feel the edges of forgiveness; for holding on, for letting go, for giving, for taking so little. We're not to blame. The pictures are all wrong.

WE ARE ALL SEATED AROUND THE TABLE with the feast laid before us. I am at the head with Nellie at the other end. To my left is Sophie, with Simon seated between her and Sid. Vinny, on my other side, sits next to Clara.

The table is covered with Sophie and Clara's creation. It is, as Vinny predicted, a beautiful thing. Held together by thin strands at some places and wide swatches at others, it dangles and drapes in an unexpected elegance. Vinny said it's minimalist in nature. Then I said it's animalist and then Vinny said that wasn't funny.

We are all dressed in our finest wears. I have showered for the first time in what seems like years. Nellie played with my hair for half an hour, perfecting every curl, and then I put on my white nightgown with tiny pink flowers. Nellie said we would pretend it was a formal gown and she puffed up the sleeves, straightened the ruffles. She unfastened the first button and played with the collar ribbon until it fell just right. She is wearing what she calls her traveling clothes: blue jeans, a T-shirt, and work boots. It's not fancy, she told me, but she did wash out the shirt.

Sophie and Clara, who spent the day shredding, must have rolled in the dust from the fabric. They both seem to glitter, their eyes reflecting the sparkle. Simon has scrubbed himself down to an ivory white and both Sid and Vinny are exceptionally well groomed. Vinny, as usual, appears to have donned a tuxedo for the affair. He looks particularly dapper this evening and I tell him so.

"Thank you, my lady," he says with a gentleman's nod, "and you are a vision in nightwear."

"It's a formal gown, Vinny," says Nellie, in keeping with our agreement.

"Of course it is," says Vinny, diplomacy worthy of the international circuit.

"A lovely setting," says Sid.

Nellie smiles as she stands to light the candles.

"Ooooh," says Simon, "pretty."

I reach for Vinny's plate, intending to begin serving the roast but am stopped by a single haunting note from Clara. I am compelled to set down the plate and bow my head. We sit, all of us, silent and in awe as Clara sings grace. As her last note disappears into the darkness outside our circle, we raise our heads.

"Thank you, Clara," I say.

Simon slaps the table in appreciation. "Pretty," he says.

"Yes, it is," says Nellie to the bear, which sends both Simon and Clara into a bout of shyness.

I pick up Vinny's plate and serve up the meat. It is perfectly done and the smell of it has us all slightly agitated, having lived on Spam for so many days on end.

"Not too rare, please," says Vinny.

Nellie has taken up doling out the side dishes: mashed potatoes, a vegetable medley, fruit Jell-O, cucumber salad, and creamed onions.

"More please," says Simon as she dollops the second heaping spoonful of mashed potatoes onto his plate.

"Why don't you finish this and then we'll get you some more," she says.

Simon nods his big head fervently. I slice tiny little pieces off for Sophie and Clara although I'm certain they could shred this just as proficiently as they did our tablecloth. As her plate is set before her, Sophie leaps straight up and lets up a howling meow. For a split second I am alarmed and then I realize she's simply an excited cat. In fact, as I take in the table as a whole, I see several excited cats, tongues licking chops, paws and claws poised to bat and skewer.

With full plates in front of each of us, Nellie stands. She raises a glass of sparkling melted snow. "I want to make a toast," she says.

"Here, here," says Vinny, and he extends a paw toward his glass.

"To you"—her glass is tipped toward me—"who, by way of your great courage and determination, have brought us all to this moment."

She raises her glass as a chorus of meows and one appreciative growl ring out. Nellie puts the drink to her lips, giving the signal to everyone else but me to step onto the table and begin lapping from their glasses.

"Thank you," I say and I, too, drink to the toast.

"We must eat now!" shouts Simon.

I raise my fork and the meal begins. Simon dives directly into his plate, huge paws shoveling in massive bites. Sophie pounces onto the meat, batting it wildly, flinging it into the air, howling screams of joyful play. Clara chews and hums at the same time. She makes the happiest melody I have ever heard her sing. Not even Sid and Vinny make an attempt to maintain our formal setting. They gobble at record speed.

Nellie and I watch the mayhem, we are human observers. Then we give a nod to each other and forgo our silverware, with fingers we pick up our meat, swipe up our potatoes. Vinny is the first to return for seconds, opting to eat directly from the platter this time.

We gorge ourselves on a never-ending supply of food. It doesn't disappear. We wish for more and there is more. Simon eats a full roast all by himself. It seems like hours before the orgy slows. One by one, we fall away, sliding to the floor in exhaustion, stretching out full to accommodate our stuffed bellies. The cabin is abuzz with moans and sighs as Vinny, the last to fall, joins us on the floor.

"I haven't given my toast yet," says Vinny, trying to sound alarmed but without the energy to back it.

"Well, we haven't had dessert yet," says Nellie, and the room lets out another groan.

"I think a short nap is in order," says Vinny.

I am about to second his motion when an enormous belch shakes the cabin. Simon is deep in sleep, snoring and burping, making the string from the roast that hangs from his mouth sail up into the air.

———

SLOWLY, THE SHARP PAINS IN MY STOMACH SUBSIDE and I drift somewhere between sleep and wake. The snore of the crowd around me acts like a lullaby. I don't know how much time has passed when my eyes open. The floor of the cabin is rumbling, an unfamiliar light is coming through the windows. I drag myself to the door, open it.

Now I am standing in front of the cabin. Vinny and Sophie are at my feet. We are watching the horizon. It is a rainbow of color, a moving stream of tiny little dots: red, orange, yellow, green, blue, indigo, violet. We watch as it begins to move away from the horizon to our right.

"It's coming toward us," Vinny says, and I realize he's right, using some kind of theorem from tenth-grade geometry.

Snow covers everything for as far as I can see but I'm not cold. I look down at Sophie and Vinny. They sit calmly, tails wrapped delicately around tiny feet. It's obvious that they, too, are not cold.

I look up and the dots are closer, moving with remarkable speed. They are so close now that I can see from where I stand that what is coming at us is a remarkably long caravan of brightly colored pickup trucks.

"They're all pickup trucks," says Vinny.

"I know."

We look at each other with a simple regard. We look back to the caravan and the first truck, a vibrant blue, is coming to a stop only some five or ten feet away from us. Behind the blue truck, a green one, then a red one, then yellow, then hundreds and hundreds in more shades of more colors than I've ever seen.

The door of the blue truck is opening. I see a foot stretch down to the ground. Then from around the door, a woman appears. She is a statuesque glamour girl, long blond hair, skintight gold dress.

"Look!" says Vinny. "It's you."

"Yeah, right!" I say, smiling wryly.

I glance down at Vinny to show my appreciation for his joke and he is looking up at me with earnest green eyes. I turn back to the woman and look straight into her face. To my delighted surprise, there is a striking resemblance. Then at her heels is a cat, a sturdy-bodied calico with a mischievous glint in the eye.

"It's you, Vinny!" I exclaim, certain beyond any doubt.

"Where?" he says, eyes darting past the calico, looking for another.

"Right there." I point to the playful calico.

He is shaking his head. I look back to the glamour girl and she is coming toward me. Then following both the girl and the calico is a little orange cat.

"It's Sophie!" Vinny and I shout in unison.

Sophie recognizes herself immediately with a quick hop and an arch of her back. This cat is her, fur for fur.

Now I am seeing the trucks empty out, one behind another. From the green truck steps a plump milkmaid complete with muslin dress, white cotton apron, and wooden pail. At her feet, a cranky Siamese and then a little orange cat.

"There you are again," Vinny and I say to each other as I point to the Siamese and he points to the milkmaid. Sophie hops up again.

The red truck delivers a woman in black leather, bound in chains, brandishing a whip. I am tempted to run, her presence is so daunting. In her train, an enormous red tom and a little orange cat.

A line is forming, led by the glamour girl, who now stands before me. Her cats stand before Vinny and Sophie. She extends a hand toward me and finally I recognize her, recognize me, the glamour girl. Mute, I take her hand and we shake. Inside, I feel a smooth calm. I see it in myself; a tiny globe filled with mist and breeze and sun, swirling around together, passing through each other slowly and steadily, constantly moving.

The glamour girl's calico extends a nose to Vinny, who responds by extending his own. They touch, nose to nose. Sophie has immediately begun to clean between the ears of her little orange cat.

Then I am shaking hands with my milkmaid, thinking of an old boyfriend who once said, "You look like a milkmaid and when you smoke, you look like a milkmaid smoking." Vinny greets his Siamese. Sophie cleans Sophie.

Then the leather queen steps forward. My apprehension dissolves as our hands touch, my fear of her confident authority turning to admiration. I look past her at a line of me and Vinny and Sophie that extends farther than I can see. I'm an old lady, a crippled girl, a middle-aged housewife, a trapeze artist, a woman in a suit, a man. Vinny is a longhair gray, white Persian, enormous Maine coon, tiny brown. Sophie is Sophie, a little orange cat.

The procession continues past us, filing into the cabin after each has extended a hand or a nose or an ear. With every greeting, my smooth calm grows. I glance down the line and see a fuchsia truck unloading a human-size black-and-white cat. In the enormous cat's trail, two cat-size cats.

"Vinny," I whisper, and nod toward the startling sight. Vinny studies the scene.

"Perhaps it's your inner kitty," he says, and quickly turns his attention back to the part of himself that stands before him.

Before me stands a man, blond and tall, prepster good looks. I am stunned and I pause before offering my hand. This is not me, I think, this is Ray. He smiles at me, holding out his hand steady, gentle. Then I realize that it is me and Ray. Then I realize that, in fact, it is just me. It is the part that he changed in me, that I changed in him, the part I gave away, the part he left behind. I take his hand and in it I find resolution, a physical thing, come from the body. I feel all that I gained from knowing him, loving him on whatever level it might have been. Grief gathers in my throat, so many remnants both missing and gathered. I open my mouth and the sadness ascends in a mist. I look him in the eye. We are equal, we are both forgiven for all we did and didn't do.

Then I begin to see in each of the dimensions not just me but the influences of me. I shake hands with my mother in me, my father in me, with the boys who ratted me out for pulling down my pants in the bushes, with my grandfather, with skinny little Carol Bacon in her Danskin, with Kate and her cigarettes. I even shake hands with the sniveling Four-Square weenie, Donna Perkins.

The globe of smooth calm has grown beyond me. It now holds me inside it. With every handshake, every acceptance, it inches out that much farther. It takes in Vinny and Sophie, the cabin, the trucks. The smooth calm is everything I see.

As the last in the line of us passes by, we turn and follow them inside the cabin. We are a full house, crammed to the gills. Everywhere I look, sleeping mes, Vinnys, Sophies. We search, each of us, for a patch of floor and join the slumber.

A CLATTERING OF DISHES RATTLES ME AWAKE. I have no idea where I am. I search the room for clues and see the multitudes. Slowly, I remember the celebration dinner and Nellie and Sid and Clara. I look at the clock by the window. Three hours have passed. The sky, plastered with stars, sends a glow through the cabin.

Nellie, making no note of our new guests, is setting the table for dessert. She is stunning in the star glow.

"I passed out," I say, hoping to confirm that what I have just had is a dream, though evidence to the contrary roams freely through the cabin, albeit at a safe distance from the original clan.

"We all did," she says without looking up from her work.

I continue to scan the room. My clan has rallied. The cats

are roaming about; Sophie and Clara bat a dust ball back and forth, Vinny and Sid are investigating dessert, and Simon sits at his seat, ready for more.

"Ready for cake?" Nellie asks me.

She looks up from her work and there is something different about her. Her image is sharper, clearer, even more familiar than I remember. I imagine the sound of a Xerox machine enlarging its focus to 152 percent. I try not to stare.

I sit up on the floor and say, "Always ready for cake. Will you help me to my chair?"

"You can do it," she says.

I am stunned at her refusal. A flash of anger hits me in the head and Simon suddenly bolts up. I look him in the eye.

"I'm afraid that I won't be able to," I say, and Simon sinks back into his chair. Then, by myself, I wiggle to my chair and pull myself up, rung by rung, until I am sitting in my place. I am a child smiling, pure pride.

"Ice cream?" Nellie asks.

"Just cake! I made it to my chair," I say.

The best piece of chocolate cake I have ever seen is set before me. Vinny makes a gruff sound as he clears his throat, moves to his seat, nods to me a greeting.

"I'd like to propose a toast," he announces, and everyone hurries to their places.

Vinny steps up onto the table and sets himself in a tall, elegant form, tail wrapped around paws. Again he clears his throat.

"Our journey was born out of innocence," he begins.

I bow my head, happy and contented to be listening to another of Vinny's distinguished ramblings.

"Our lady put us in the car and we beat a steady path north." He is nodding and, being the adept public speaker that he is, making eye contact with everyone at the table.

"Although I did not know why at the time, I soon came to

understand that we were on some sort of a quest. My immediate assumption was that it was her quest"—he nods toward
me—"and as events unfolded, my certainty of that fact grew.
Being the simple cat that I am, I did not see my own opportunity as it lay before me."

There is a shift in his tone, I am startled and suddenly not
so much at ease. I look up, around the table, we are held in
an unexpected suspense. I look at every face, each one fixed
on Vinny. For the first time, I have no sense of what he will
say, of what he is thinking. He has changed in the last several
days and now I am acutely aware of a distance that feels like
it has only just begun. From here it will grow.

"Not until the arrival of you"—he nods to Nellie and Clara
and then to Sid, where his focus remains.

Vinny's eyes bore into Sid, who sits at full attention. He
alone seems at ease with Vinny's speech. I am filling with an
anxiousness, a dreading that I am about to lose something,
someone. It dawns on me that this was never to be a celebration feast. It is a farewell dinner.

"You entered our cabin with a knowing command. I didn't
recognize it at first, was unnerved by it, even frightened. I saw
a true leader of quiet wisdom. Something I have never been
able to be." Vinny pauses for a moment.

I am shocked at his words, that I had no inkling of all that
he felt.

"But as the days passed, I came to know you," he continues,
"and only today did I finally come to realize who you are."

I am transfixed and completely lost. I stare at Sid, waiting
for his response. I feel woozy and incapable of understanding.
As I stare at the tiger-stripe cat, he slowly shuts his eyes and
lets his head fall into a single nod. I shift my focus to Vinny.
He nods back.

"You see," he says, "my wish had been for our lady."

He turns his focus to Nellie. "For you."

Nellie nods. Clara and Sophie are nodding. I am out in the cold. Everyone is nodding but me.

"I knew what I had wished for her; for her to see herself more clearly, to see what others see. But for myself"—he stops and shakes his head in wonder—"I had dared not think that I was ready for such an awakening, had no idea what might follow."

I am still back on his confession, his wish for me. He wished for me to see myself. Looking at Nellie, my focus sharpens yet again. She no longer looks familiar. She looks like a reflection.

Vinny is standing now. He says, "But lo and behold!" and then he walks toward Sid, they stare into each other's eyes, and then Vinny says, "Like all successful quests, you simply continue forward until you are in the place where the answers find you."

Sid leans forward and the two cats touch noses and I see what I have seen so many times before; Vinny looking in a mirror. I see Nellie now, not sitting at the other end of the table but standing next to a green truck at the very end of a long procession line of me. The cumulative result of my hundreds of dimensions that are standing at attention along the walls of the cabin, she is as close as a reflection can be.

Now Vinny turns to Sophie and lowers his head. He sinks into his front legs. He stays in this position as Sophie cleans between his ears. I realize that he is bowing to her, giving her his greatest esteem. I am trying to piece this together. If Sid was his awakening, then Sophie is somehow what comes next. I am confused and dazed.

Vinny raises up from his bow, says, "And now I would like to dance."

He moves to the edge of the table and jumps down. There is a lightness to him that I don't recognize. He moves to the middle of the room and stands very still. Then in a sudden gesture, he is airborne. He stretches up toward the stars, then arches in midair, turning gracefully downward, landing on his front paws. Then he is running in a circle, bigger and bigger, building up speed until he cannot help but extend into a breathtaking leap, fully outstretched. He begins to howl, then screech, ever twisting and turning. Sid leaps from the table and, without a hesitation, they are a single movement.

I look to Sophie, she has jumped to the floor herself. Clara is at her side, her mouth fully open. The song has begun and Sophie and her Clara have joined the celebration.

As I watch them dance and sing—Sophie, Vinny, Clara, and Sid—a brightness rises up from the floor and, finally, I see. It has been Sophie, all along, who has held the secret; to be lost in love, to dance or sing with joy, to live where there are no doubts, no questions of identity, who she is or how it happened. To be orange and small and to never want for tiger stripes or thumbs.

A gust of wind pulls my attention to the door. There Simon stands, a silhouette against a dazzling starlit blizzard of snow. The bear turns to me and cocks his head. Then, without another gesture or a single word, he turns and walks out the door.

"Simon!" I say, but my plea can barely be heard.

"It's all right," says Nellie, who is suddenly at my side.

The door stands open and I watch as my big bear disappears into the swirling whiteness. I turn to Nellie and see her fully revealed.

"He belongs out there," she says. "The snow will keep him safe."

Then she holds out her hand and says, "Dance with me."

"I can't—," I say, and then I know that I can and slowly I do.

I stand for the first time. She holds me and we sway to a music that falls through the air. Through the open door, the blizzard blows into the cabin. The howl is so piercing a sound that it turns sweet inside my ear. As the snow whips around our home, it starts building drifts against our walls, pushing my dimensions closer and closer to me until I feel them falling into place, within me. I am filling up.

I can barely see through the white now, only the occasional paw or tail as it leads or follows a leap through the air. I have lost Nellie in the snow but still feel her hold, keeping me upright, and then I know that her hold is beneath my skin, she, too, settling to that place that had been so empty.

I hear bells peal sweetly as the final piece of my puzzle finds its place. I have been, for so many years, just outside myself, a place made solely of sight and sound. Only as I sense the strangeness of Nellie settling inside me, taking space that was so long used for my arsenal, do I realize what a long time I have been here, standing outside. Watching all of it. Feeling none of it. Another dimension all along, I think, and then I resist looking around for the pig who had startled Sophie.

I squint against the wind, turn to look in each direction, but I can't see anything but snow. My cabin is lost in the blizzard and I know I will never see it again. Hurling through space, wishing for oneness, it had appeared as I had needed it, a safe place in which to move toward peace. It was my capsule, my protector, but now I have broken through the atmosphere and air is everywhere. I have made a successful reentry.

I feel Nellie smile, happy to finally be at home. I hear her in my mind.

"Snow is like love," she says, "it's pure. It's beautiful when it first falls but it so easily disappears. So many things must be in perfect harmony for it to stay, to keep it from ice, to keep it from rain. It's a magical balance but if you can find it, it will stay forever."

Then her grip begins to relax as she lets go and finds her

place among the many mes, finally all with the room they need to sit comfortably. I feel their confidence, my own, that they will be accepted but not held, able to come and go, ever redefining.

I am standing of my own will, holding myself up from the inside at last. Resolution is a physical thing. I know this now for certain. It has come from my body.

I dance to the sweet flight of an oboe as it rides over strings in a growing swell. My white flowered gown twirls around me and I know that we have broken free. We have leapt beyond the "wait and see," we dance in a blizzard with another, in whatever form that may take. Flying through an unknown cosmos, without a hint of fear. There's evolution in the air, thick as gravity. I see it like a sunrise. I hear it like a crescendo.

"Do you think I'm a girl?" I hear Nellie asking.

"Without a doubt," I answer.

"Do you think I can love?"

"Yes."

"Home free . . . ," she says.

I look down at my legs, watch them dance. I see Nellie's work boots. They are her feet, they are mine. It makes no difference. From inside my flowers, I stare at my work boots and see everything else that sits in between, everything a perfect fit.

Vinny's very first wish sounds in my head. "I have always thought so highly of you and have always wished you thought more highly of yourself."

Music permeates my whole body, it wraps around me. Space is expanding, filling with snow. The blizzard whips me round and round. I feel a hand in my hair, a hold on my waist. I see my own hands moving to the line of my form. I feel skin against skin, a curve for a curve, then a kiss.

"If we can love today, we can love tomorrow," Nellie says.

"And if the snow melts," I say, "it doesn't mean it didn't fall."

"But wouldn't it be nice if it stayed," I hear her say.

"It's something to wish for," I whisper.

I take myself by the hand and spin me into the blizzard.